WRESTLING

WITH

Your Angels

WRESTLING

WITH
Your Angels

A SPIRITUAL JOURNEY TO GREAT
WRITING

JANET O. HAGBERG

Adams Publishing
HOLBROOK, MASSACHUSETTS

Published by Adams Media Corporation
260 Center Street, Holbrook, MA 02343

ISBN: 1-55850-496-6
Printed in the United States of America

First Edition
J   I   H   G   F   E   D   C   B   A

Library of Congress Cataloging-in-Publication
Wrestling with your angels: a spiritual journey to great writing / Janet O. Hagberg.
   p.   cm
Includes bibliographical references.
ISBN 1-55850-496-6 (pbk)
1 Authorship   I Title
PN145.H27   1995   94-46802
808'.02—dc20   CIP

This book is available at quantity discounts for bulk purchases.
For information, call 1-800-872-5627.

*Just as there is that critic on one shoulder,
there is an angel on the other shoulder,
whose only goal is to help
your writing take on its greatness.*

*This book is dedicated to Barry
and to all the writers
I have worked with, for they
have taught me well.*

Contents

Acknowledgments

My angel and my inner critic took me on a journey as I wrote this book. My angel taught me to speak boldly, even when I wanted to back away. My critic held off with his critique until after the first few drafts were finished. I am grateful to them both. During the writing, I suffered a serious, computer-related physical injury and I wondered if it was a message to stop writing. My angel convinced me of the opposite, that it was a message to take care of myself while writing. I didn't stop writing and now I am relieved that I didn't. I am well and the book is finished.

There were, of course, many people involved in the birth of this book. I would like to thank Ellen Hawley, editor of *A View from the Loft,* the literary magazine of the Loft, who first urged me to write essays for her and then challenged me into a book. She is the midwife of this project. I am indebted to all the writers I've worked with at the Loft and in spiritual direction, who have inspired me, put their souls on paper, and allowed me to use their writing as examples. My thanks also go to David Kolb, whose pioneering work on learning styles I adapted for the Learning Style Inventory. My dear friends and family have been supportive of me and of this book, even when I've been discouraged. They kept me going on this important journey.

I am grateful to many more people, who helped me in the process of editing and publishing. First, colleagues who read the manuscript and gave me valuable feedback; Bobbie Spradley, Roseann Lloyd, Jill Breckenridge, Pat Weaver Francisco, and Lillian Eggers. My agent, Malaga Baldi, gently led the process from raw manuscript to contract completion and beyond. And my editor at Adams Publishing, Laura Morin, guided the book ably through the publication process. Lastly, I acknowledge my gratefulness to the Holy, from whom I got the vision and courage to embark on this book.

Prologue

This book is about soul writing—the writing that emerges when we find our voice, take the risk to expand to our full potential as writers, and tap into that deep place within us where both pain and passion dwell, which is only accessible by facing our fears and wrestling with our angels.

Soul writing is a spiritual process, a process which leads us into intimacy with the holy, creative essence and with our own souls. I call this essence the Holy, and I believe it is beyond us and seeks to dwell within us. Other people use different names for the Holy, names like higher power, God, Sophia, or the universe, but the spiritual journey to intimacy is what is crucial—the treacherous, exciting, and awesome journey that takes us to our spiritual core, our center, then takes us beyond that to places we never knew before. As writers, we must be willing to go on this journey in order to find out not only who we are at our core but to find our deepest heart's desire, our passion, whatever we are called to write. When we heed the call of the Holy to follow our passion, the writing that emerges is courageous, fresh, truthful, and compelling.

The soul journey is a sacred journey that needs to be taken both seriously and lightly. We need to dance and play, nurturing ourselves on the journey, as much as we need to listen and discipline ourselves. Intimacy with the Holy allows us to do both simultaneously. The soul is the essence of who we are, our own humanness, our own individual spirit, our own unique promise of possibility.

I believe the spiritual journey leads us to great writing in two ways. One is by leading us to our authentic voice and our fullest potential as writers. We come to this by understanding our strengths as writers, accepting our voices, and stretching ourselves to become fuller writers. I describe this way in the first two sections of the book. The second way is a more profound way but also more treacherous: it involves embracing our inner critics and wrestling with our angels. I describe this in the third and fourth sections. This way requires us to take that inner journey to our essence, our core, where we come face to face with our fears. It requires that we go to the place where both our pain and passion dwell, but where freedom also reigns. The result of that struggle is a gift, unique to us as writers.

Soul writing is this gift—our unique passion in writing, our calling.

Throughout history, writers have given many names to the creative force that leads them. Muse, mystery, spirit, force, and inner light are just a few. I use the word angel because it goes beyond the idea of muse for me; it includes a spiritual component, a holy element that seems more powerful.

I use the term angels broadly in this book. It can mean inner voices or images (the accumulation of positive figures, loving people, self-esteem); real people in our lives who love us and act in the role of angels; spirits of people who have died but who are present as benev-olent beings; and other spirit forms who are messengers of the Holy. The role of angels in our lives is equally broad. They are guardians, supporters, encouragers, warning figures, messengers, protectors, assuagers of fear, wrestlers.

Soul writing begins when we set aside what we think we have to write in order to be good writers, when we let go of other people's opinions, and when we quit comparing ourselves to everyone else, negatively or positively. Soul writing has a chance to develop when we lay aside the excuses, the expectations, and the false impressions and take a spiritual journey through the unknown.

Developing soul in writing is not easy. It is a process that takes us to new places. To develop soul, we need to concentrate on our spiritual journey. We need to question our culturally accepted practices. Instead of trying to shut down or destroy our inner critic, we need to become intimate with it and embrace it. We need to let our writing take us deeper, to places we would rather not go, knowing that in this process we will learn to trust our inner voice, face our fears, gain intimacy with the Holy, and invite courage to be our constant companion. In doing these things, we make our writing process sacred.

Most writing classes and hundreds of books teach people the craft of writing: metaphor and description, texture and infrastructure, char-acter development and dialogue, point of view, plot, grammar, and sentence structure. Still other books concentrate on ways to start writing, ways to keep writing, ways to choose new content, ways to get published. These are all necessary to the writing process, but they do not get at soul writing.

No one can teach soul writing directly. All one can do is create an atmosphere which honors the process of soul writing and encourages writers to wrestle with their angels. When I teach writing, I concentrate on soul for three reasons: First, it is the most difficult aspect of the writing process to embrace, and I like challenges. Soul writing invites writers to continually go deeper into their psyches and dig for the essence of their writing. To paraphrase what Annie Dillard says in *Teaching a Stone to Talk,* the deepening experience asks them to ride their monsters down to their core, to find the center where both pain and passion reside together. I can't provide that atmosphere unless I am willing to ride my own monster to my core.

When I rode my monster to the depths, I found emotional and psychological abuse I had long denied. But as a result of that journey, my writing and my creativity flourished. The energy bound up in denial of pain was now free to create, and I was free to teach without the fear of facing other writers' monsters. Before that time, when I touched on soul with students, I would either revert to technique or simply not encourage the student to go deeper. I was afraid to either go with them or guide them on the inner journey. I didn't know if I could go where the journey would take us.

The second reason I concentrate on soul is that I believe it is the component most lacking on the literary scene today. It can take a thoughtful story and turn it into great writing. An example is Jung Chang's *Wild Swans.* The book is technically and structurally interesting, its content is compelling, and it is alive with spirit. But that alone does not transform the book. As I read it, I felt that Jung Chang's soul was in it. She had passion for this story. It moved her to her core. I became aware of her possibilities.

The third reason I concentrate on soul is that it brings me to my knees. I am always humbled in the presence of courageous writing, passion that breaks the rules, of writers who look into the face of fear and keep writing. When I see writers who can confront the truth of their lives and write with non-degrading humor, who can write well-crafted fiction with a message, who can break through to new forms of poetry and essay, it awes me. It keeps me in touch with my own soul.

Soul Transforms Writing

Let me tell you a story of how my own soul encounter affected a class I taught recently. I walked into the first meeting of my writing class, "Wrestling With Your Angel," to find fifteen eager and anxious faces looking at me. As we introduced ourselves, I had my own usual anxieties: Who were these students? Would they trust my philosophy of writing? Would they trust themselves? Would anything miraculous happen?

Most of the students had introduced themselves by the time we came to Bob. He had difficulty speaking due to a harelip, but he braved it, and the class listened intently. We went on to the next person and finished the introductions. On the way out of class, Bob handed me a column he had written for his neighborhood newspaper. I thanked him and left.

On the way home, I thought about how different this class might be with Bob in it—how much more I would need to listen; how the other students might react. That afternoon, I worked on a book dealing with leadership, in which I encouraged leaders to engage with people who were different from them, people from whom they could learn, and let those people be their mentors for a year. It occurred to me, in a blinding glimpse of the obvious, that Bob was just such a mentor for me and that he was in my class to teach me, not for me to teach him.

I wrote Bob a note thanking him for the article and encouraging him to keep writing and to come back to class. He did. And he wrote stories week after week, asking me to read them to the class. One story was about sharing something with his sister for the first time; another described how he was a gift to his parents. The other writers responded positively, both to Bob and to the class, and everyone kept writing. On the fifth week of class, Bob asked me privately if I thought it would be all right for him to make ceramic angels for each class member. Guessing how much personal time and love would go into this project, I could feel tears of gratitude welling up in me. I said I thought it was one of the most profound things he could do.

When the class members received their ceramic angels the next week, they reacted with numbed silence, then with profuse thanks. Each of them told Bob how special this class was because of his presence and generosity. I noticed a heightened sense of caring and courage in the students' writing. A few miracles even occurred. One woman wrote for the first time about having been born "illegitimate"; another wrote about unresolved grief. Two published but blocked writers found new book topics and began writing first drafts.

This class was about touching soul—my soul. If I had not heard my own soul speaking to me about Bob, I do not think Bob would have been as free to write about his sister and parents, nor would the other writers have been as free.

Touching our soul in writing is an inner journey, and it happens best in an atmosphere in which the soul is honored, the writing is deemed holy, and the ground—no matter how much it quakes—is experienced as sacred.

Reading This Book

I have organized this book around four major themes, which are also the four sections of the book: "Listening to Your Voice," "Honoring Nurture and Discipline," "Letting Your Writing Take You Deeper," and "Listening to Your Spiritual Calls."

You may want to skip around in your reading. If you have already experienced and appreciated your authentic voice, then skip to another theme and start reading there. If you are good at support and discipline but want a breakthrough in your writing, go to the third section, "Letting Your Writing Take You Deeper." I mentioned two ways to develop great writing. The external, more technical way is described in the first two sections; the other, more internal way is described in the last two sections. Listen to your inner voice and let it direct you as you read. Experience the book as part of your spiritual process. Let it emerge, call to you, engage you. Trust yourself and what you are attracted to in each chapter.

At the end of each chapter, I have included several exercises for you to try. The first set of questions leads you more personally into the content of the chapter. The second set is made up of writing exercises. The third set is visual, for people who learn well by drawing or making symbols for their ideas. The fourth set provides guided imagery to take you deeper into yourself and into contact with the Holy. You can use these sections on your own, as discussion topics for writers groups, or as teaching tools in writing classes. Try to experience them as part of the spiritual process of soul writing, not just exercises to complete. Listen when you write. Write with your own voice, from your own soul.

Now begin the journey to your soul. I hope you enjoy the book and that your soul is touched in the process.

Letting the Spirit Work in Writing

I am not solely in charge of my writing. Sometimes I think I am. That's when I've let my mind take charge. Each of us is a mental, physical, emotional, and spiritual being. Yet when I approach writing, I frequently limit myself to the intellectual or the emotional realm.

If we are open to our whole selves, I believe we will come closer to our truth and increase our confidence in writing.

I will describe a spiritual approach to writing. For many writers, I will be simply naming experiences they recognize but have not been consciously aware of before.

Spirituality is an intimate connection with a power beyond us which seeks to dwell within us. Spirituality involves the way we live out our response to that power, the Holy, who invites us to take a courageous inner journey to a place we have never been before. Spirituality has been described by many writers. Rilke exhorts us, "Nobody can counsel and help you, nobody. There is only one single way. Go into yourself. Search for the reason that bids you to write." L'Engle says, "Artists must be open to their shadow side, the wider truths, the strange worlds beyond." Blake describes imagination as the divine body in everyone.

I believe that spirituality in writing means honoring the holy, creative essence beyond us and dwelling in us, and letting our writing process reflect this. This is a journey we embark upon voluntarily.

Ultimately, the spiritual journey is about intimacy with the Holy, which takes us to our passion and to our deepest heart's desire.

When I first felt compelled to write what was in my heart, even though I had no way of knowing whether it would be published, I knew spirituality was at work in my writing. All of my books have been written before they had publishers.

Writing what is in my heart is not easy. A few years ago, I began writing a book on leadership. Part of my research included a trip to the West Coast for interviews, but after the first few I was frustrated with the responses I was getting. Midway through the trip, a college mentor whom I interviewed said, "I think it's great you're doing this, but it doesn't seem like your heart's in it."

She was right. I was pushing the book. I went home, put my notes away, waited several months, and began writing a book on spiritual development, which has since been published. I wasn't ready to write a book on leadership yet. I wasn't sure what I wanted to say. If I had written it then, it would have been a very different book than it later became.

Let me describe and illustrate four ways in which spirituality influences our writing. These are four phases of the spiritual journey to great writing and they are the four themes of this book.

Listening to Your Voice

It takes courage to trust your writing voice, because everyone else's voice is different than yours. As writers, we are buffeted on all sides. Teachers critique our work or tell us to read other writers; editors cross out our words; we lop off whole paragraphs ourselves. How do we sort out who we are from the writers all those other people want us to be?

Finding our voice is a sacred experience, requiring respect for ourselves. If we connect to a trusted power beyond ourselves, we can more confidently sort out our voice and style. That doesn't mean we can't improve or change by listening to other people. We can. But other writers will simply inform our writing, feedback will give us choices, and editors will give us another perspective, not remake our writing or silence our voice. To be useful, feedback must move us closer to our own essence, our core, our truth, our story.

Questions that might lead us to our voice include:

- What is in my heart to write?
- What does this feedback tell me?
- What questions does this work raise in me?
- Is my writing honest?
- What parts call for change, inclusion, deletion?

In a writing class I taught at the Loft, a large, nonprofit literary organization in Minnesota, we each wrote and read something aloud so the other members could describe, not evaluate, our voice. We used descriptive words like precise, cautious, funny, sad, angry, persuasive, personal, cynical, rather than evaluative words like wonderful, dull, good, perfect.

One class member, Carol, read a memoir. The words we used to describe her voice were clear, straightforward, cynical, humorous, angry. After class, Carol wanted to talk to me. She said she felt stuck in her angry voice. I asked what was happening in her life. She said her brother had died suddenly six months ago, but she thought it was too depressing to write about. I told her that avoiding this writing might be why she was feeling stuck. If the time was right, she could let her angry voice rant and rage about her brother, using her journal if she didn't want anyone to see it. Eventually, she would be able to move on to other topics and would feel freer to develop her humorous views of life. She was relieved and went home to write.

Pauline didn't want to read her work to us. She said it was because she was boring. The class encouraged her to read and let us decide if we thought she was boring. She read a piece about her high school piano teacher, who was the first Minnesotan diagnosed with AIDS. Her piece held the poignant discovery that she was in love with him. She opened her memoir, "I awoke with a tightness in my throat. The kind that you get when you try to hold back tears that don't want to be held back. I had just had another dream about Bruce. I began to go over the details only to be sharply brought back by a cold voice from within saying, 'He is gone. He is dead. Let him go."

Rebecca, a professional speech writer, brought another issue to class. She liked her job but was frustrated because her own voice was lost in her professional role. She explored various writing forms in class—poetry, travelogue, fantasy. We encouraged her to honor her voice in her professional writing as well and see what happened. She thought it would be impossible, but she tried. She wrote strong feelings and opinions into a speech on a topic close to her heart. Her boss loved it and it was picked up by newspapers around the state. She later wrote, "I got the confidence to be influential in my speech writing. My attitude made the difference."

A friend of mine, Barb, who is a professional writer, was astonished when she began writing poetry. What emerged was a voice from deep within her but of a different culture. She has written a series of powerful poems exploring religious themes and self-concept. She is amazed at the insights she gets from these poems and she honors this voice, even though it is inexplicable.

Honoring Nurture and Discipline

My own writing process calls for equal amounts of nurture and discipline. Other people need a different mix. As writers, knowing the mix and getting it are vital to honoring our process.

I have friends who nurture themselves by writing in their favorite restaurants. I write better in quiet places with my twenty-pound cat, Moose, and my herb tea nearby. The crucial thing is to find out what feeds our writing and to set up that environment. I call it making the space sacred, whether that means lighting a candle, taking a walk, sitting in a favorite chair, or looking out a window. Discover *your* inner needs. Once we know the nurturing place, we can hear what our writing wants from us.

Alice Walker, the author of *The Color Purple,* described her frustration in starting that book. Her characters would not reveal themselves to her while she lived in New York City. As soon as she moved to the country, they began speaking. We can't all move to a different location to write, but we can be more aware of the environment in which we write.

Discipline is the other side of nurturing. It involves setting aside time and creating space in our lives to write. It's about taking ourselves seriously as writers. Do we deserve the time? Does our writing warrant the time? We need to keep saying yes, because even when we don't believe it, the creative essence beyond us does. We have to give the spirit room to work.

Set aside time to write every week, even if it is only fifteen minutes at first. Different times of day work best for different people. Even if you just sit, think, or watch the squirrel outside, it is time spent on the writing process, time spent taking the time seriously. In *If You Want to Write,* Brenda Ueland says, "You will sit before your type-writer or paper and look out of the window and begin to brush your hair absentmindedly for an hour or two. Never mind. That is all right. That is as it should be—though you must sit before your typewriter just the same and know, in this dreamy time, that you are going to write, to tell something on paper, sooner or later."

Writing simmers longer in some people than others. While one person is writing first drafts on paper, another is writing third drafts in his or her mind. We're just different that way.

A graphic example of discipline comes from Jean, the mother of an active five-year-old, and pregnant when she started my writing class. We skipped one week's class for a holiday. During that week, Jean delivered her baby and returned to class the following week. She was determined to finish class and keep writing. Now she's in a group called Mothers Who Write, which meets on Saturday mornings. She writes during her infant's nap times.

Letting Writing Take Us Deeper

Whenever fear threatens to stop our writing, we can choose to lean into the fear, face it, and let it take us to a new place, a deeper place. Keep listening to your writing. Let it sit and read it again. Ask what it wants next. Ask yourself: are my feelings alive in this writing? What am I holding back? Would another form be more powerful for this content? Where is the truth in this piece?

The most difficult turning point for me and for my students is the time when we must choose to go deeper or stop. We all have strong inner crit-ics standing on one shoulder, reminding us of our failures, telling us to stop before we embarrass ourselves, showing us "good" writers, and telling us not to plumb our depths because it will be too hard, too gruesome, too boring. Robert Bly said he wrote about things that were outside himself until he was forty-six. That's when he faced his grief over his father. After that, he wrote about his insides and his poetry took on new life.

If on one shoulder we have a critic, on the other we have an angel (muse, mentor, friend, spirit, source), providing answers to the critic. We need to believe the angel's answers and practice this side of the dialogue with the critic over and over: "I write because I want to tell this story. I have a right to my voice. I like to write. This is what I want to say. I'm sorry you don't like it. I'm not writing for you. Quiet down so I can write."

Going deeper requires taking a plunge. We must respect the sacredness of our process, our voice, our courage, our core, and write what comes, in the form it emerges.

Tish came to class very tentatively the third week. She said she'd been writing at home while she was in a bad mood. She wrote for an hour into the darkness she was feeling. To her surprise, on the other side of the darkness emerged a letter to a childhood friend, Annie, about their first tap dancing class. The sounds of her tap shoes, "Shuf-fle ball change, shuf-fle ball change," had the whole class smiling. The letter turned into a story series that she sent to her friend, reconnecting them in a new way.

Amy brought to class the idea that good writers should write serious fiction. Yet she was drawn to writing about the ways her young children saw the world, and her views on controversial issues. She felt energized by writing nonfiction. Everyone encouraged her to write what she felt, and she has published several pieces since then. One piece, "Possibilities vs. Babies," said, "Quite simply, I do not regard fetuses as babies—little people. I consider them as amazing possibilities. When I mourned my early miscarriage, I was not mourning for a real baby, but for that particular possibility of a baby. The miraculous combination of tissues growing in my body had the possibility of developing into a human being, but much could happen—and did—before that occurred. The sadness I felt at the time has been completely overshadowed by the intensity and joy of birthing two real babies."

Her energy emerged in this piece. Her style is engaging partly because she is the loving mother of two children writing on the difficult topic of abortion. She had found her writing voice.

Alan read the class a story about encountering a Native American whom he stereotyped as a drunken Indian. As he wrote, he discovered that the story was more than a casual look at a person he thought of as different from himself. The man asked him if he was Indian. Alan denied it, although in fact he is part Native American. Alan wrote:

> I realize I am unwilling to be identified with this drunken Indian. I am unwilling to admit we are of the same blood, the same genetic material.
>
> We are that, and more. The same genetic material, the same emotional material, the same spiritual material. Much more than blood connects us. I, too, am an addict. I know what it means to drug feelings of worthlessness that never seem to go away. Buddy, we are more than blood brothers. We are brothers in pain. The thoughts come and I feel a strange sort of affection for him. I see warmth, friendliness, intelligence. In other circumstances, I think I would like him.
>
> "No," I say again. "I'm not Indian." He reaches out to shake my hand. "You can be Indian," he says. "It's okay."

It is difficult to write honestly about our issues, personal crises, strengths, pain, disappointments, isms, strong beliefs. But when we listen carefully to our inner truths, we discover new depths in ourselves and in our writing.

Listening to Our Spiritual Calls

Spiritual calls come from the Holy, frequently in the form of nagging inner requests. Somehow these are easier to respond to than writing blocks, but the two are not unrelated. Writing blocks are the special property of spirituality in the writing process. Maybe they appear because we could be doing something different than what we think we should be doing.

Rather than trying techniques to break through these blocks, we can ask what else we might write or do. A poem may want to be born before the next chapter of a book is written. A story may want to be a poem, or a poem may want to be a book and it won't be happy until we honor the wish. Sometimes the story, poem, book, or essay doesn't want to emerge at all.

When I acknowledged being blocked in researching the leadership book, I was led to a totally new book. It was hard to close the door on the book I had in mind, but it was the right thing to do.

Whenever we feel blocked, on a small or a large scale, we can ask what the call is. Our spiritual essence knows and will inform us if we ask.

- Do we need to write more clearly?
- Do we need to change our point of view?
- Do we need to change the form?
- Do we need to be bolder?
- Do we need to tell the truth?
- Do we need to let go of something?
- Do we need to end the story?
- Do we need to get feedback?
- Do we need to stop getting feedback?

Kate wrote a story about a girl named Molly who wanted to explore a seashore. When she became stuck in the early drafts, Kate decided to ask Molly what was bogging the story down. Much to her surprise, Molly told her. "I want you to write with a bright pink pen. And I want you to write in my words, not your words."

Kate obeyed. The story took on a youthful, fun-loving style that Kate and Molly both enjoyed.

This chapter was originally an essay, and it was written in response to a spiritual call. I rarely write essays, and it was risky writing for other writers. I am not a glutton for punishment. I was afraid I would be criticized for describing the spiritual dimensions of writing. Writing about this mysterious process is not logical, critical, or academically sound.

However, spirituality works for me and for other writers I know. I draw from my spiritual source for essays, poems, nonfiction books, even mysteries. Sitting down to write this, I got out my fountain pen and legal pads, made a pot of my favorite tea and turned on the telephone answering machine. I asked my holy muse to give me the courage and grace to say what was in my heart and honor the writers whose stories I've told.

Halfway into the first draft, my critic got active. I put on warm clothes and took my regular two-mile walk. I walked out on my critic. It doesn't like walking. As I walked, I asked for guidance for the next steps in the essay. The nagging thoughts disappeared. I returned to my draft, revitalized. It's refreshing not to be solely in charge of my writing.

Reflecting on the Introduction

1. What is your definition of spirituality?

2. How does your spirit affect your writing?

3. What gets in the way of deepening your spirituality?

4. Which parts of the spirituality of the writing process are you most attracted to? Why? You might want to read that section of the book first.

Writing Exercises

1. What do you most enjoy reading?

2. What do you most enjoy writing?

3. When do you first remember loving to write? Why?

4. What seems to get in the way of your writing?

5. What questions do you have about writing?

6. What are your goals in reading this book?

7. If you were to take your spirituality more seriously, what do you think would happen?

Visual Exercise

Draw your spirituality in a symbol, picture, or word. Draw yourself into the picture. What meaning does this have for you?

Guided Imagery

Go to a quiet place in the center of yourself and rest there for a few minutes. Let yourself be aware of a presence around you that is safe, warm, and sacred. Imagine that presence surrounding you and then whispering in a quiet voice, "I am asking that you go on a journey with me to a wonderful place. But in order to do so, you must be willing to take a risk. Are you willing to do that?" Be still and think how you will respond. Answer the holy presence and tell it why that is your answer. Then come back to the present and write about this in your journal.

ONE

~

Finding Your Voice

Voice is at the heart of all writing. We can learn all the techniques available and write in all forms or genres, but if we are writing from someone else's voice it will sound forced and inauthentic.

In *Writing Without Teachers,* Peter Elbow says, "In your natural way of producing words, there is a sound, a texture, a rhythm—a voice—which is the main source of power in your writing."

According to Elizabeth Winthrop, voice is an author's way of telling a story. In *The Writer,* she says, "You know it when you have it and you often suspect when you don't, but you don't know how to make the leap from one state to the other. When you've found your voice, I think it's like a rider finding his seat on a horse. Your legs are pressed against the horse's sides, and you and the horse move as one. When you have found your voice—your way of telling a story—you and your book are in concert. You move as one. That's the best way I can find to describe the feeling."

Yet how many of us, when we hear other writers reading their work, feel envious or critical of ourselves or of the other writer. At our core, we have a difficult time accepting our own voice as valid. Many writers search their entire writing lives for someone else's voice, a mentor's perhaps, or a famous writer's. So one of the most difficult spiritual passages for a writer is to find his or her voice.

The reason for the difficulty is that finding our voice means writing from our soul. If we can go to that place within ourselves to start writing, whatever we write will sound authentic, real, convincing. For me, the most important part of the writing process is finding the inner place from which to begin.

The only challenge more difficult than finding our voice is appreci-
ating it. Many writers think their voice is inadequate or wrong, so
they try writing in their most difficult voice, thinking that what's difficult must be good. As a result, their writing sounds strained and their
own voice is demeaned.

Write the Way You Speak

The best advice I was ever given as a writer was from an early mentor. It was simple and straight forward: "Write the way you speak."
What he was telling me was not to take on the words or characteristics of people I thought I should write like, but to say things the way I
would naturally say them. If I did not use long erudite words in
speaking and used them in writing, I would come across like someone
who was trying too hard. If I spoke in short sentences rather than
compound ones, but used paragraph-length sentences in my writing,
it would show. If I spoke in strong, direct language but used "may"
and "sometimes" when I wrote about controversial subjects, I would
give mixed messages.

Writing the way we speak means writing as naturally as we can.
Some writing teachers recommend speed writing as a way to get to
natural writing, and that works for a lot of writers. Another method is
the spiritual approach, which I describe later in this chapter.

It also helps to listen to your own voice reading your writing out
loud, just to yourself at first. When you get braver, read to other people—classmates or friends. Just for fun, try writing like someone else,
a well-known writer for instance, who writes differently from you, and
read this out loud. Notice how strained it sounds.

Part of writing the way you speak is noticing what topics you speak
about. If you are interested in—or angry or curious about—something, it is a clue to what will drive your writing. Many aspiring writers went to James Michener to find out how to write. He always
asked them the same question, "What do you have passion about?" If
they could think of nothing, he said he was unable to help them learn
to write. His belief was that you could teach the techniques of writing
but they would do no good to a writer who lacked the passion necessary to sustain and fuel the writing.

The artist Vasily Kandinsky wrote, "That is beautiful which is produced by internal necessity, which springs from the soul."

Every voice is unique. Every voice has something valuable to say. The challenge is to find your own and not borrow someone else's, thinking that the other person's voice will make you a better writer. As you accept your own voice, it will begin to sound more authentic, undiluted. Then it may surprise you and expand, or leap to another place altogether.

I have selected several pieces by my writing students to give you a sense of the range voice can cover. As you finish each segment, ask yourself how you would describe it and check the possibilities I have suggested. Then ask which voices attract you the most, how you feel when you read them, and which is most like your voice. There are no right or wrong voices, just different voices, but we are attracted to certain ones. That is why we read the things we read, and write the way we write. Try to quiet your critic as you read and appreciate your own rich and unique voice.

The first voice is Tom's, telling us about his thoughts during a frightening experience.

The Waiting Room

One floor below, my sister lies asleep;
Her opened body hopes to find and keep
Freedom from the menace lurking deep
Within the dark. I wait here with the others
Whose loved ones also sleep beneath the knives,
That cut through flesh like smooth and graceful swimmers
Who stroke through blood to rescue drowning lives.
I stand and, through a window, I can see
A pool of water set into the earth.
A fountain rises from it, tall and free;
Jetting high, it forms an arcing path,
Then pauses, crystalline, before it falls.

I take a breath and ponder love and fate,
Then turn to sit once more with those who wait.

Now check the words that describe this voice and add your own.

serious _____   humorous _____
angry _____   sad _____
hopeful _____   intense _____
joyful _____   relaxed _____
direct _____   subtle _____
abstract _____   visual _____
sensuous _____   tactile _____
persuasive _____   cynical _____
thoughtful _____
others _____

The next selection is from Chuck, who writes about a group of young boys. In this excerpt, they get a chance to go to a Native American Sun Dance with a local Indian named Bones and the father of one of the boys. When the adults want to go off to party, the boys are left with an old Indian named Victor Threefeather. He is speaking.

"That over there," the old Indian said slowly. "Sad." He paused. "Supposed to be a prayer. You see?"

"Like church?" Dick asked, puzzled.

"I been to your churches. Not like that. Prayer. To be, should be prayer."

Dick persisted. "That's our church—pray and stuff like that. That's what they do."

Then Dave and Al chimed in. "Yeah, that is, that's—"

"No. Prayer. This dance is a three-day prayer. You pray, I heard your prayers. Not a minute. Phht. Gone. Quick as a fart in a windstorm is a white man's prayer.

"But it is not a prayer no more. They drink, all drink, damn stuff you bring."

"We bring?" Dick asked defensively.

"You—big you, not little you."

Dick asked, "Do Indian kids have t'pray for three days?"

The old Indian was puzzled.

"Boy, my knees'd really get sore," Al chirped.

"Mine too," Dick added.

"Why would not they dance three days?" asked old Victor.

"No, pray three days," Dick repeated.

"Dance is pray, pray is dance. I have seen your prayers—on your knees and reading it, all oratory. We dance."

"Do Indian kids have to go to church every Sunday?" Dick asked.

"Church—no. Sunday—no. Only those who are poisoned by the white father-reverends. Indian-kids—Indians do not."

"So they don't have t' go to Sunday school?" Al chirped again, excited now.

"Not—no," the old Indian stammered.

"Wow!"

"Keen!"

"Neat-o! I wanta be an Indian," the boys erupted.

"Ha. Not when I tell you an Indian goes to church all the time. All day."

"Huh?" the boys chorused.

"What makes you think the Great Spirit listens to all those words? The Great Spirit does not speak to *you* in words, why do whites think the Great Spirit speaks your English?"

"I never heard God speak nothin'. They say at Bible school he talks to people, but I never heard nothin'," Dick said disgustedly.

"Me either," the others repeated.

"Ha, you don't listen. Follow me up the Big Medicine Mountain. You listen."

Now check the words that describe this voice and add your own.

serious _____	humorous _____
angry _____	sad _____
hopeful _____	intense _____
joyful _____	relaxed _____
direct _____	subtle _____
abstract _____	visual _____
sensuous _____	tactile _____
persuasive _____	cynical _____
thoughtful _____	
others _____	

Roberta gives us the next selection, which is an excerpt from a poem she wrote while on an inner journey.

Depression

Here it comes again
the shadow of a cat
slipping in
between body and soul.

The cloudy membrane
over the cateye
that shades the look
of everything.

The sticky humidity
clinging to its coat
that permeates every pore.
Sniffing around for
the tantalizing scent
of seduction gone sour.

The stray
curls up
around the heart
and claws it to shreds.
Leaving the remains
to slowly putrefy.
Its toxins absorbed
into the system.

The feline's presence
harmless as mist
and as bone chilling.
Its breath
warm as desert heat
and as dehydrating.
Its body
the color of burnished lead
and as crushing.

Innocuous but terrifying.
Is it what I allow it to be
or does it have
a life of its own?
Rendering me helpless
in the face of gravity.
A losing battle
the downward spiral
sylvan slippery
purring
numbing.

Now check the words that describe this voice and add your own.

serious _____   humorous _____
angry _____   sad _____
hopeful _____   intense _____
joyful _____   relaxed _____
direct _____   subtle _____
abstract _____   visual _____

sensuous _____   tactile _____
persuasive _____   cynical _____
thoughtful _____
others _____

The last selection is from Stephen, who had the experience of staying with six sled dogs during a three-hour layover in the middle of a race in which his wife was a musher. The story takes place on a cold Michigan night, with blowing winds and freezing rain howling across the football field which serves as the rest point. This excerpt comes from a scene in which he has become aware that the youngest and most inexperienced dogs are restless and starting to move around. River, a small, reddish husky with a white stripe down her head, stands and looks towards the starting gate. After a moment, Mac rises up on his front paws and stands up too. Kido opens his eyes next. In a moment the whole team could be up when it is so important that they sleep. A team of older dogs would know to rest, but aside from Barney, these are all yearlings, inexperienced.

> Without thinking I very slowly stand and walk along the team, Barney, Bo, and Kido watching me, their weight shifting onto their front shoulders.
>
> Reaching the front tire of the truck, I kneel on the ice-covered parking lot and lie flat back onto the straw between River and Mac, resting my head on the big truck tire, my shoulders on the straw, my boots flat on the pavement, knees up to keep my legs off the ice.
>
> I put my right arm out across the straw, reaching towards River, but not lifting my hand off the ground. She stands for a second, then folds herself back down onto her bed, her back pressed up against my arm. She is warm against me, and I press gently up against her. As I do, I hear a sigh on my left as Mac circles down again. I reach out my left arm to him and he rests his chin on my hand.
>
> Lying in the middle of the team, my body a bridge between dogs, I sense all six closing their eyes again against the blowing wind.
>
> The gusts blow sheets of freezing rain onto my face, turned up and exposed to the night sky, and all its elements. My hood has shifted back on my head as I lie against the tire, laying my brow open to the sky. My face runs with the water blowing against it.
>
> River's constant pressure against my arm is like a hug. Dogs never place their weight against you without intention. Mac gently turns his head left and right, rocking his chin on the back of my hand, forming a hollow in the thick fleece protecting my hand.
>
> I realize that my hood is back from my face, but don't really consider doing anything about it.

I am open to every element of the night, and I briefly marvel at the sensation of peace I feel. When we are in the world, not a thing apart, no element is hostile unless we fail to love enough.

But the marvel passes, for the source of that marvel is the very ordinariness of this communion I share with the night, the wind, the cold, and my brothers and sisters lying with me in gentle fellowship.

Now check the words that describe this voice and add your own.

serious _____	humorous _____
angry _____	sad _____
hopeful _____	intense _____
joyful _____	relaxed _____
direct _____	subtle _____
abstract _____	visual _____
sensuous _____	tactile _____
persuasive _____	cynical _____
thoughtful _____	
others _____	

Spirituality and Voice

Finding our voice is a sacred experience, requiring respect for ourselves. We need to understand that our voice is a gift from the Holy and that our voice is unique to us. If we trust the Holy as giver of this gift we can more confidently sort out our voice and style. Our job is not to negate or abuse our voice but to recognize, appreciate, nurture, and honor it. Yes, and trust it as well.

One ritual that will take you to your authentic voice is going to that quiet, deep place within you in order to start writing. For some, this means walking in nature; for others, sitting quietly. Go to that quiet, grounded place and ask the Holy to give you your gift of voice. Then ask for the courage to accept and respect it.

Voice has both an inner and an outer dimension. The outer is our style, our way of writing or telling a story. So far in this chapter, I've focused on that aspect. The other dimension is the inner voice, the message giver, the nudger, the guide, which we experience as critic or angel or the Holy. We need to learn to listen to our inner voice and decipher its messages, both positive and negative, then learn how to respond in ways that enhance our writing. I describe that process in more depth in chapters eight and nine.

What our inner voice tells us is that we were put here because we have something to say. Our purpose as writers is to find out what it is and say it in our own voice. Some people like to have an affirmation of this. Ancient Hebrew scripture gives us such an affirmation in these words:

"And I have put my words in your mouth,
And hid you in the shadow of my hand."
ISAIAH 51:16

If it helps to have these words indelibly written on your heart, memorize them and repeat them several times before you begin writing. If other affirmations work better for you, use them.

Finding and honoring our voice is really about self-acceptance, self-love, and accepting unconditional love. When we've learned to honor our own voice, we appreciate voices that are different from ours and respect the uniqueness of a wide range of voices.

My voice has emerged in a way that now satisfies me, but it took me quite a while to acknowledge and respect it. I would describe it as direct, strong, vulnerable, humorous, persuasive, sad, practical, energetic, angry, serious, hopeful.

From time to time, I have wished for a different voice but now have come to feel affection and camaraderie with my voice. It emerges in all the forms I write in, even though at first I thought I would need a different voice for different forms. I was surprised, when I began writing fiction, that I still had the same voice—my voice.

My voice is most stimulated by questions I can't answer. That is the motivation, the starting point, for most of my writing. I love to probe mystery, to uncover my truths. The writing helps me to find answers for myself and to share them with others. My voice helps me share the process, the concept, the story, the results.

I have written a set of guidelines to help myself keep track of and honor my particular process, which I have honed over twenty years:

1. Write what's in your heart, whether it is popular or not.
2. Listen to and respect your muse.
3. Write the way you speak, especially in first drafts.
4. Let the writing guide you.
5. Write to probe questions, probe yourself, and probe mystery.

6. Give time and fresh air to your writing.
7. Nurture your inner source of inspiration with retreats, play, classes, reading, travel, and support from other writers.
8. Be open to the unexpected and the unexplainable.
9. Detach from money as a major issue in your writing.

I have also written a purpose statement for my writing: The purpose of my writing is to be faithful to the Holy and to probe mystery.

You may want to write your own guidelines and purpose statement. They can help you keep your sense of direction.

If you are still uncertain of your voice, the next chapter, "Learning Styles and Writing," will assist you, in a more technical way, to describe your voice. I invite you to try it.

Reflecting on the Chapter

1. How would you describe your own voice?

2. Does it feel like a gift? Why? Why not?

3. What are your writing guidelines? If you have none, write some.

4. What is your purpose statement for your writing? If you don't have one, try writing one.

5. Do you understand voice as a spiritual idea? Why? Why not?

Writing Exercises

1. Write on this question twice, once in a happy voice and once in an angry voice. Then combine them. Question: What do you wish you'd told your mother?

2. Have a dialogue with the body parts you don't like. Look back at your writing and describe your voice.

3. React to this statement: You are here because you have something to say. How do you respond? What does it stir in you?

4. Write about the color orange, or green, or purple. What voice elements come forth as you write about what this color touches in you?

Visual Exercise

Draw your voice in animal form. What animal most reminds you of your voice? Why?

Guided Imagery

Go to a holy place in your imagination. Look for your voice in all the corners or cracks or drawers in that place. Search around for your voice. When you are tired, sit down and rest. Be aware of a voice from behind you saying, "Your voice is not to be found in the drawers or the corners or the cracks. Your voice is inside you. I put it there. Use it. Honor it. Listen to yourself." Let that message sink into you and sit quietly as you ponder its meaning. Return to the present and write about this in your journal.

TWO

Learning Styles and Writing

Finding our own voice means writing from our soul. If we can go to that quiet place at the center of our soul to start writing, whatever we write will sound authentic and convincing. For me, the most important part of the writing process is finding the place inside me where I can begin.

In the last chapter, I wrote about the spiritual approach to finding your voice. There is also a very practical way to understand your voice: by understanding the four learning styles. Several years ago, I developed a learning style inventory for my career development work, and it dawned on me that there might be a correlation between the way we learn and the way we write. I tried the learning inventory out with my writing classes, applying each learning style to a distinctly different writing voice, and found that once writers discover their most comfortable styles, their voices are freed.

If you would like to find your own learning style before you read about how styles apply to writing, turn to the end of this chapter and complete the Learning Style Inventory.

Learning Styles

Learning is the process we use to take in information of all kinds—to sort it, make sense of it, and give it back to the outer world. You can think of learning style as a futuristic computer, one into which you can put sounds, shapes, tastes, colors, textures, smells, moods, letters, temperatures, and feelings. Once the information is inside, the computer, which is our mind, uses our learning abilities to mix it all together, make sense of it, transpose it, and send it back in the form of ideas, speech, words, symbols, facial expressions, models, and body movements that fit together to form a whole.

Figure 1 describes the four learning styles. They are: enthusiastic, imaginative, logical, and practical. We all have the capacity to learn in all four ways, but each of us has a strong tendency toward one style, which is our best and easiest way of learning. All four styles are equal, though different, and all can be used successfully in writing.

You may find yourself identifying with more than one style, because we often combine two or more in order to write effectively. But try to isolate the one style that describes you most.

The two styles on the top of the grid, enthusiastics and imaginatives, learn best through their feelings, whereas the two on the bottom, practicals and logicals, learn best through thinking. Enthusiastics and practicals are action oriented in their learning, whereas imaginatives and logicals learn by watching or observing.

How might these different learning styles look in real-life situations? Let's take skiing as an example. The enthusiastics jump on their skis and head down the slope, probably screaming as they go. They may fall, but they are likely to meet someone as a result and will have a great story to tell.

The imaginatives find someone who knows how to ski and they watch for a while, absorbing the techniques. They may follow the person down the hill and imitate the moves until they get the feel of it. Then they're off on their own.

The logicals think ahead (they always do) and read up on skiing before they go, so they won't make fools of themselves. They bring all the right equipment. The challenge for them is to put their knowledge to work.

The practicals want to know just one thing before they go: How do you stop these things? Once they know that basic principle, they experiment with different techniques, probably coming up with a new way to ski.

Can you imagine an enthusiastic having to read a few books on skiing before trying it, or a practical following someone without knowing how to stop? Can you imagine a logical jumping spontaneously on skis the first time out, or an imaginative conjuring up the principles before following someone down the slope?

It seems ridiculous, but when people write, they often try to be the opposite of what they are, because they think it will make them better

Feeling

Enthusiastic	Imaginative
Gets involved with lots of new activities; is good starter	Sees lots of alternatives, the whole picture, the gestalt
Operates on trial and error, gut reaction	Uses imagination
Gets others' opinions, feelings, information; depends on them	Creates with emotions, aesthetic interest
Involves and inspires others	Is oriented to relationships with people; supportive
Searches, seeks out new experiences	Uses eyes, ears; listens, observes, asks questions
Likes risks, excitement, change, incentives	Observes others; can model behavior
Dislikes routine	Can imagine self in different situation
Adapts to situations well	Is unhurried, casual, calm, friendly; avoids conflict
Is willing to try, jump in	Feels timing is important; can't push until ready
Can be impulsive	Likes assurance from others
Learns with people through projects, discussion, doing	Learns by listening, then sharing ideas with small number of people or by modeling

Doing ——————————————————————— Watching

Practical	Logical
Applies ideas to solving problems	Is good theory builder, planner
Makes theories useful	Puts ideas together to form a new model
Has detective skills, searches and solves	Synthesizes
Tests hypotheses objectively	Is precise, thorough, careful
Is unemotional	Can organize; follows a plan
Uses reason, logic to meet goals, take action	Redesigns, retests, digests
Speculates on alternatives	Calculates the probabilities
Likes to be in control of situation	Reacts slowly and wants facts
Sets up pilot projects, research opportunities	Works independently, thinking, reading
Acts independently, then gets feedback	Avoids overinvolvement
Uses factual data, books, theories	Pushes mind; analyzes ideas, critiques
Is responsible; takes action on tasks	Is rational, logical, complete
Learns by working at probabilities and testing them out, coming to conclusions	Learns by thinking through ideas and designing a plan or model in an organized way

Figure 1   Thinking

writers. Enthusiastics try to be logicals, imaginatives try to be practicals, and so on. If we want to add other styles, it's best to wait until we are very comfortable with our own style and voice.

I am a practical learner. This shows up in all of my writing. I write to explore ideas, solve problems, answer questions, and develop models. I am not strongly drawn to metaphor, sensuous image, and beautiful description, or to the structure and pattern of a piece, although I have learned over the years how to work with each of these. They just don't come easily to me, so they are not the backbone of my writing.

A few years ago, after twelve years of writing and three nonfiction books, I wanted to branch out. I explored several forms and was most attracted to suspense fiction. Now I know why: As a practical learner, plot attracted me. Not all mystery writers concentrate primarily on plot, but all mysteries *have* a plot. Who did it and why? Characterization and description were new for me, but I was willing to learn them because I knew I could concentrate on plot. I had more fun writing that first mystery than I could have imagined, and I think the challenge has made me a more confident and versatile writer. But the base of that confidence came from recognizing my best learning style and honoring it, no matter what genre I was working in.

Enthusiastic Writers

Enthusiastic writers concentrate primarily on feelings and experiences. Their affinity for experience comes alive as they describe feelings and events. In fact, just the act of sharing their writing is helpful to them. They are probably the group that most enjoys open readings.

Enthusiastics can start a story spontaneously and let their characters grow before their eyes; they can talk to them, feel their feelings, let them go off in different directions. One of their best traits is the ability to heighten the feeling tone of a piece.

Their advice to others would be, "Trust your gut." Most of their writing is personal, whether it takes the form of fiction, poetry, or nonfiction.

For enthusiastics, the writer's journal is important. They write pages and pages and use their journals as a source for their writing. They may also benefit from having a tape recorder close by, because they have spontaneous ideas and feelings that are lost quickly if they are not recorded.

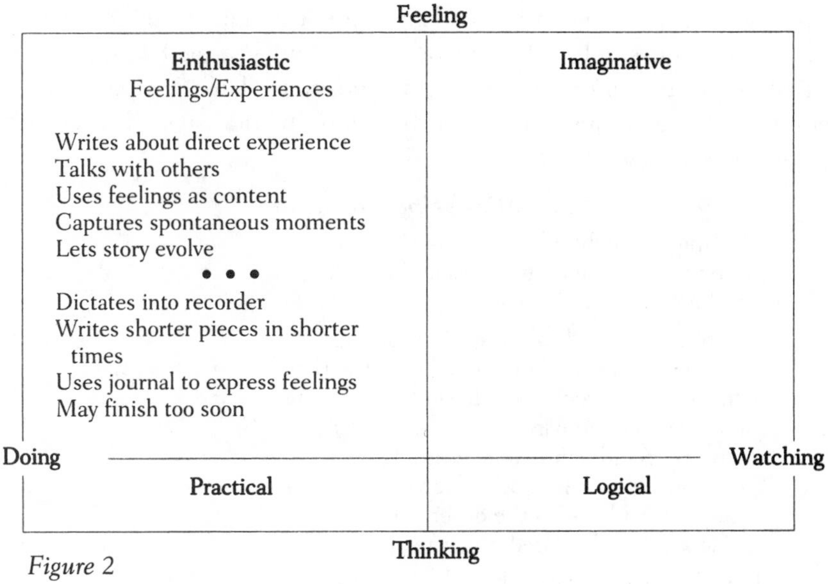

Feeling

Enthusiastic Feelings/Experiences Writes about direct experience Talks with others Uses feelings as content Captures spontaneous moments Lets story evolve • • • Dictates into recorder Writes shorter pieces in shorter times Uses journal to express feelings May finish too soon	Imaginative
Practical	Logical

Doing ———————————————————————— Watching

Figure 2

Thinking

What enthusiastics want to know from other writers is when they can meet next and share stories about their writing experiences. Writers' groups provide them with variety and stimulation; they also help them to polish pieces, which can be difficult for them.

Shorter pieces attract enthusiastics, because they are action oriented and like to move on the next project, whether they have finished the last one or not. They seldom need to write multiple drafts, which would stifle their enthusiasm, although they can benefit from constructive feedback.

Enthusiastics do not mind the business end of writing—publishing and promoting—as long as they can do most of it orally or through personal contact. Networking comes much more easily to them than to other styles.

I asked a friend, Roseann Lloyd, author of *Tap Dancing for Big Mom,* to write four poems on the same subject as exaggerated examples of each writing style. I wanted to show how people with different learning styles would approach the same subject—through choice of words, use of metaphor, shape of poem, and feeling tone. The subject for all four poems is a recent controversy in Minnesota: the storage of nuclear waste in dry casks on land. After much public debate, the legislature voted to allow it. The seventeen steel casks will be located on Prairie Island, in the Mississippi, just south of our city, Minneapolis. This first poem is an example of the enthusiastic poem, Roseann's natural style. The poem's focus is the feeling experience of the writer.

The Mississippi in Spring

Walking up the bluffs above the river
there was nothing between us and the sky
but the wind, glorious wind.

When we looked down, the Mississippi,
far below us, seemed more a lake than a river
with its inlets, creeks, and bays. At floodtime,
the river's high, moving up into the trees.
Lush waterland, a breeding ground
for herons, mallards, frogs. The vista
so huge, the bluffs on the other side
seemed to be a hundred miles away.

Two blue herons came flying by—mates.
They floated easily, turning south then east,
graceful, in synch, scalloping
the sky. Playing, they seemed to turn
only for the sake of turning. Then they rode
the updrafts, rising steadily, then falling,
to turn up again. At last they headed north,
still in tandem, a wing span apart.

My heart stopped at the thought
they were headed for Prairie Island,
seventy-five miles from here. Would they build
a nest in the shadow of radiation? Would
their eggs break open before their time?
Would their babies come out deformed, eyes
bugging crooked, beaks curling back
into their necks?

The day was so beautiful,
it seemed like nothing dangerous
could be close at hand. I stood
on the bluffs above the river, somewhere
between land and sky. I imagined the invisible
radiation gone. I imagined beautiful
windmills on the bluffs, here and across

the river, making a clean harvest
of the wind.

The sun was on my face, and the wind.
May it always be strong, the herons rising
with it, and their young.

Imaginative Writers

Imaginatives are most attracted to images and visuals. They see life and story scenes like snapshots in their minds, and all they have to do is describe them. They register the smells, sounds, tastes, colors, and textures that go with a piece of writing. They live inside their writing and get the sense or feel of a piece before they write it. They often write several drafts in their hearts before anything comes out on paper, so their first draft is like the fourth draft by a writer of another style.

They are drawn to metaphor, analogy, and simile. They make rich use of imagery and often love a piece primarily for the wonder of its description or images. Their motto is, "Show, don't tell." Books thicker than two inches are usually written by imaginatives or logicals.

Imaginatives store descriptions of people, places, and things for later use. They may notice an unusual scene and not know where it will fit, so they write it down and put it in a file. Two stories later, they pull it out and drop it in, and it fits perfectly.

The relationship of writer to writing is an important issue for imaginatives. It is sometimes hard for them to release their thoughts to paper, and some great stories or images get locked inside forever, never sufficiently developed to come forth. Their internal critic informs them of the need for perfection, but getting the piece on paper quickly often helps them stifle the internal critic.

What they want to know about other writers is who they are, how they live, what they do to develop their craft. They may not need to meet them; reading about them may be sufficient.

The business side of writing is least interesting and most difficult for them. A mentor or agent may be more important for them than for some other learning styles. In fact, having another person to report to regularly helps imaginative learners. They need support and encouragement to complete their writing, but they usually shy away from large groups.

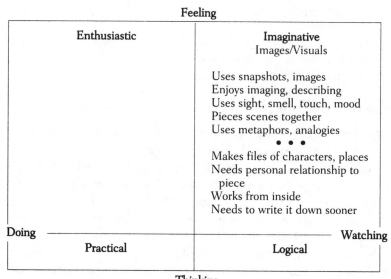

Figure 3

This second poem is an example of the imaginative style. The images and metaphors are the body of the poem.

Radiation

We lay down with death
and he did not become our friend.
Ruthless, he ran with the power we gave him,
his arms long, his fingers stretching,
his claws sharpened
on this new bright energy.

He extended his reach
into a hundred centuries
rather than a single one. War
became his second favorite toy.

His jowls grew fat, his gums bloody,
his belly extended
from his opulent feasts.

There he is by the river, humming,
swinging his scythe,
his white cloak blowing in the wind.

He is so fat from eating, he staggers
like a drunk.

He walks alone, now
that we are gone.

How necrophilic we were
to lie down with death

to give death
so much sway.

Logical Writers

Logical writers concentrate on facts and structure. They enjoy planning and organizing their pieces. The infrastructure of the piece intrigues them—the names of chapters, the lengths of sentences, the shapes and the rhyme schemes of poems, the names of characters. It is the skeleton upon which they hang the words. They like the patterns as much as the writing process, or maybe more.

"Think it through" is the motto for this style. Logicals think ahead and are great researchers. They gather the facts, and readers can be sure the facts are correct. They don't enjoy making things up as much as they enjoy finding things out. They can sustain their writing over long periods of time, and they too can write two-inch-thick books, but they are usually detail oriented, rather than image oriented. You know the exact color and origin of the rose, not just that it heralded summer. Logicals love to teach through their writing.

These writers know where their writing is headed before they begin. They use structure and outlines as their guides. For this reason, they are good at writing publishing proposals. They can write articles on many subjects, because they do not have to love the topic to research it and have fun with the writing.

What they would like to know from other writers is what books on technique and research they find most valuable. They love learning more about the facts of writing; that and a good dictionary will make them happy. They usually don't go to writing groups. They spend that time doing research. A regular call to a writing friend is sufficient.

For them, the issue is finishing. There are always more facts, better words, unexplored ideas. They can tolerate producing many drafts in order to find the right words, but they have to put limits on their work so they

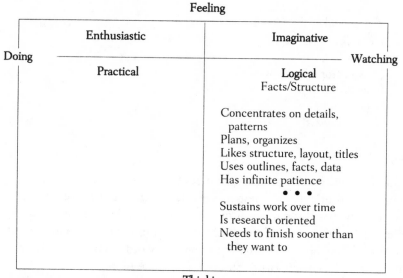

Figure 4

can move on. Strict internal editors sometimes hamper logicals, because they find it hard to generate the spontaneity that helps get a piece started.

This third poem illustrates the way a logical might take on the topic of nuclear storage, using facts to illustrate the danger.

The Radiation in the Seventeen Steel Casks

will be alive for 10,000 years.
During the lifetime of our children, it will be alive,
living out its unnatural life by the river.
And during the time
of our children's children, our grandchildren.
And their children: our great-grandchildren.
And so on. Radiation lives farther into the future
than we can remember backwards. Can you call out the names
of your great-great grandmothers? Radiation
will still outlive
our great-great-great grandchildren:
those who have forgotten our names—
Kantrowitz, Prescott, Stubblefield, those who
cannot read our language: neither the gravestones,
nor Mormons' genealogies

buried in the salt caves deep in Utah.
Radiation will outlive the generation after that,
those who cannot decipher the orange warning sign.

10,000 years is many generations.
So many, it would take another 294 lines
to list all our grandchildren. How many
thousands will they be?

All their lives in peril
for this generation's convenient
pleasures.

Practical Writers

Practicals are drawn to ideas and solutions. They write to solve problems, explore ideas, or raise and answer questions. Purpose in writing is important for them; they may want the reader to think about or do something as a result of reading. The impetus for their writing usually comes from an idea that nags at them or is so important they can't refrain from writing about it.

Principles and theories are important to practicals if they can make them work in real life. They are interested in how and why ideas work. This shows up in their writing process. Practicals like to explore the rules of writing, and usually change or challenge them. They are experimenters at heart and love to put ideas together differently and find alternative ways to make writing work. Their motto is, "Think and do."

Instinct helps practicals know what works for them and what doesn't. They are not afraid to put first drafts on paper and are amenable to revisions (at least a few) if they find a more useful way to say something, but they are definitely not word smiths.

Practicals are disciplined and can work well under their own deadlines. Their research files are not thick, because they count on details to come and ideas to evolve as the writing progresses. A general direction and a possible outcome are enough to get them going.

The help they want from other writers is practical or inspirational. They may go to a class or group for a specific purpose—to find help with one or two problems they were having, for example. Or they may look for an inspiring book instead, something about people who persevered in their writing through years of disappointment.

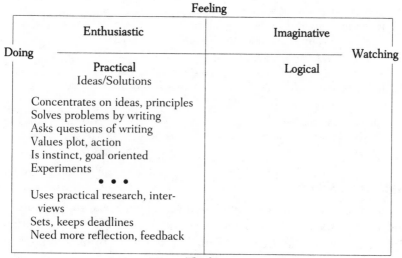

Figure 5

The business side of writing is not a problem for them, but they need editors who are able to resist becoming co-authors. They love to write for publication and can do the legwork required, even if it is not fun.

The task for practicals is learning to reflect on what they want to write. They can turn out pieces that fit a theme, but sometimes they miss a deeper meaning because of their rush to get the piece finished, or to influence someone. It is helpful for them to ask, "What is this piece really about?" It can be intimidating for them to let writing take them deeper if the task of writing takes precedence over the meaning.

This last poem illustrates the questioning approach a practical might take to the issue of nuclear storage.

The Seventeen Casks of Nuclear Waste at Prairie Island

look harmless, clean. They're polished, with a gleam.
Nobody can see the poison they emit.

That's how they want it,
the folks at NSP. Their air is clean. Dirty coal!

In short, that's the American corporate goal:
to keep everything looking clean,

even pads for women's blood bleached with chlorine.

We are so used to this cleanliness as lust,
how can we see the poisons laid out before us?
We can't see the danger in the bright red

strawberries. Clear water brings a dose of lead.
Pesticides can't be washed off, a residue like silk

on the bananas and lettuce and now our milk
comes cancerous from hormone-fed cows. We don't buy

organic, don't even complain, don't write
to Congress about banana workers sick from DDT,

coughing, old before their time at age thirty-three.
We saw it on "Sixty Minutes," had nightmares about open sores.

My landlord can't afford the same carpeting on the floors—
there's orange on the steps, on the landings, blue

but he pays someone to spray ludicrous
amounts of poison on our beautiful trees and grass.

What's the harm in dandelions? I ask.
They think I'm a fluff. I know the poisons

run down to the river, run
downstream, kill the fish—the river has a toxic hum.

What will happen in the years to come
downstream in Cairo, Illinois, when the casks begin to leak?

Has our energy dwindled, too, left us too weak
to organize? Remember the slogan *everybody lives downstream?*

Was Earth Day just a marketing dream?
Why don't we question NSP, protest at the Legislature, organize?

Again our anger and our questions are cut down to size.
"Sixty Minutes" goes to Russia,

shows Chernobyl children, sitting by diorama—
stuffed foxes, birds, painted streams, pine trees.

Their teacher tells them with a teacher's ease
what it used to be like

to walk in the woods. Yikes!
Surely the power plants aren't like Chernobyl here,

Did Mike Wallace let out a superior sneer?
It takes energy to doubt

the logic of the nuclear machine. Worn out,
enervated, overworked, we who don't see

how we can protest DDT
on bananas, who keep eating poisoned trout,

who don't call the landlord, who are bummed out
by our nightmares, how can we find a way

to protect our offspring 10,000 years away?
We can't even protect ourselves.

So What?

Learning styles are important because we can all write in all four styles, just as we learn in all four styles, but one or two come most naturally to us. It is best to start there, concentrating on what we know well, before deciding whether to branch out to other styles. Many writers specialize in only one style. It doesn't matter which we choose, as long as we are developing our own voices and not someone else's.

Now let's move on to the inventory itself.

Learning Style Inventory

Your *learning style* is the unique way in which you go about gathering information, sorting it out, and making decisions. Knowing how to use your learning style is one of the handiest tools an adult can have. You are more likely to find meaning and satisfaction in your life and work if you are aware of your best and most enjoyable style of learning.

All the information that goes into our own unique personal computer is processed in some miraculous way, using four major abilities we all possess. Each of us uses all four of these abilities in various ways and different degrees. These four abilities form the basis for our learning styles. They are the following:

Feeling: Some of us choose and digest information primarily because it feels good. We just know it when we feel it. We use our emotions to guide us in deciding what to do and how to proceed. We enjoy using body movement and speech to communicate, and we like to get involved in hands-on experiences.

Watching: Others of us use our imagination to observe and digest new materials or ideas, seeing them in new ways or drawing mind pictures. We would rather think or write about ideas, using images and analogies, than verbalize spontaneously. We like to watch other people and react to their ideas.

Thinking: Still others of us scrutinize or analyze information, pulling it apart and putting it back together in new ways. We design models and symbols, taking as much information into account as possible. What we do is systematic and reasoned.

Doing: Some of us see information as part of action, as something that helps solve a problem. We use words and actions to promote a project or forge a solution. We like to learn while doing and use learning practically. We do not enjoy learning merely for its own sake.

When we combine any two of these abilities, we get a learning style. I'll show you more about that after you take the Learning Style Inventory. But first a few words about learning styles.

- Learning styles and personality inventories are only guides to help you make the best use of your traits and preferences. They give you information you probably already know subconsciously, and should not be considered the final word on the subject.
- No one likes to be categorized. Find your favorite style, then read about the others and use them too if they are useful.
- Self-report inventories partially depend on your mood or state of mind when you take them and may vary slightly if taken at another time. Use your results, but also ask other people to give you feedback on your style.
- Your learning style may vary with the task you are asked to do, or the situation you are in. But you still have a style you are most comfortable with and in which you spend most of your time.

As you complete this inventory, pick a setting—work, home, or school. Then think of the ways you most frequently go about learning in that setting. If you are trying something new, how do you learn best? If you are preparing to teach other people about a topic, how do you most easily prepare yourself?

Mark A if you agree *strongly* with the word *on the left.*
Mark B if you agree *moderately* with the word *on the left.*
Mark C if you agree *moderately* with the word *on the right.*
Mark D if you agree *strongly* with the word *on the right.*

Begin by completing the sentences that precede each section. Check only one line per set of words.

Generally, I learn best by:

	strongly A	moderately B	C	strongly D	
Talking	___	___	___	___	Listening
Acting	___	___	___	___	Reacting
Taking small steps	___	___	___	___	Observing big picture
Being quick	___	___	___	___	Being deliberate
Experimenting	___	___	___	___	Digesting
Carrying out ideas	___	___	___	___	Thinking up ideas
Changing	___	___	___	___	Remaining constant
Being animated	___	___	___	___	Being reserved
Doing	___	___	___	___	Watching
Being goal oriented	___	___	___	___	Being process oriented
Being practical	___	___	___	___	Seeing ideals
Changing as as I go	___	___	___	___	Mapping out in advance
Finding solutions	___	___	___	___	Identifying problems
Formulating answers	___	___	___	___	Formulating questions
	A___	B___	C___	D___	

Total the number of A's, B's, C's, and D's you checked by adding the vertical columns, and write them on the lines above.

In learning situations, I am:

	strongly A	moderately B	C	strongly D	
Intuitive	___	___	___	___	Logical

Personally involved	___	___	___	___	Impersonally objective
Emotional	___	___	___	___	Intellectual
Supportive	___	___	___	___	Critical
Eager to discuss with others	___	___	___	___	Prone to analyze by myself
Interested in new experiences	___	___	___	___	Interested in new ideas, models
A believer in opinion	___	___	___	___	A believer in theory
Accepting	___	___	___	___	Questioning
Feeling	___	___	___	___	Thinking
A quick risk taker	___	___	___	___	A slow risk taker
Prone to trial and error	___	___	___	___	Prone to planning and organizing
People oriented	___	___	___	___	Task oriented
Ready to jump in	___	___	___	___	Wanting facts first
Dependent	___	___	___	___	Independent
	1___	2___	3___	4___	

Total the number of 1's, 2's, 3's, and 4's by adding the vertical columns and writing them in the spaces above. Remember, if you checked four 2's, you have a total of 4, not 8!

Scoring Your Learning Style Inventory

1. After totaling your answers, *circle your highest letter score and your highest number score. If you have ties between two scores, circle both scores. For example:*

(A 6)   B 2 ___   C 4 ___   D 1 ___
1 1 ___   2 5 ___   (3 6)   4 3 ___

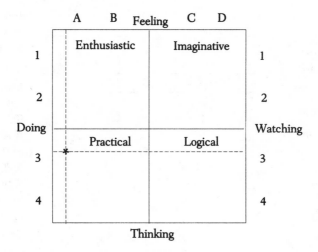

Figure 6 Sample Scoring Grid

2. Transfer these scores to the profile above, in the following way:

Draw a *dotted line down through the boxes,* starting from your highest letter score, A, B, C, or D.

Draw a *dotted line across the boxes,* starting from your highest number score, 1, 2, 3, or 4.

Mark with an *asterisk the place where they intersect.* That is your preferred learning style: enthusiastic, imaginative, logical or practical.

Learning Style: Your Scoring Grid

You have been asked to react to the four different dimensions of learning: feeling, watching, thinking, and doing. By combining these four dimensions in various ways, we come up with four different learning styles. These are enthusiastic, imaginative, logical, and practical.

As you can see from the Learning Style Grid, enthusiastic learners combine the feeling and doing dimensions of learning, while the imaginatives combine the feeling and watching dimensions. Logicals are opposite of enthusiastics, combining the watching and thinking dimensions, and practicals are the opposites of imaginatives, combining the thinking and doing aspects.

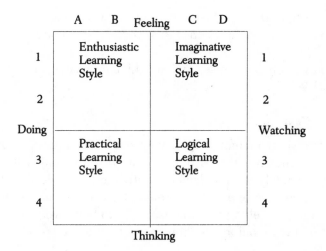

Figure 7

Some of you will have placed your asterisks in more than one quadrant of the grid. That means you either move between learning styles, are very versatile in your learning, are pressured into another style due to work circumstances, or are still uncertain of your style.

Remember, we all have the four learning styles within us. But we need to rely on our best learning style when we want to write in the most natural and authentic way. We will be both more successful and more satisfied.

Now go back to the text of this chapter and review what the learning styles mean and how to use them to enhance your writing. Once you are comfortable with your own voice or learning/writing style, you can gain the confidence to let your writing take you on a new phase of the spiritual journey—an adventure filled with surprises, which often asks you to be faithful and courageous. Go for it.

Reflecting on the Chapter

1. What is your preferred learning style? Do you think it represents you accurately?

2. How does your writing reflect your learning style?

3. Do you have the impression that you should work in another style, or that another style is better than yours? Which one?

4. If you want to stretch as a writer, which other style attracts you the most? Why?

Writing Exercises

1. Write a short memoir on a key event in your life. Now switch to the learning style that is the opposite of yours and write it again, focusing solely on the elements native to that style. Practical and imaginative are opposites, enthusiastic and logical are opposites. How does it feel to write that way? Try to honor your own learning style and voice before you branch out to other styles.

2. Write four poems on the same subject, as Roseann Lloyd did, using each learning style once. How does each one feel? Which is most comfortable? Can you accept that you have a natural and preferred style?

Visual Exercises

1. Draw your own super computer. What comes out most easily for you—ideas, words, symbols, etc.?

2. Draw the Learning Style Inventory with your style highlighted. Write several things you like about that learning style and explain why it fits you and your voice.

Guided Imagery

Go to that quiet place within you and rest there for a few minutes. Feel how grounded you are at the center of yourself. Imagine yourself in a ballroom with a large grid painted on the floor, representing all four learning styles: enthusiastic, imaginative, logical, and practical. People are standing in each grid. You move around the grid, meeting them and finding your similarities. Which group are you most comfortable with? Which are you most uncomfortable with? Sit back after you have made the rounds and reflect on the group that is right for you. Come back to the present and write about this choice in your journal.

THREE

Writing with Courage

I want to tell you a personal story which illustrates the vital role that writing and honoring our authentic voice play in the transformation process, the journey of the soul. I write this with some trepidation but with the intent of assuring other writers that moving through darkness is one way to the light and that writing is our guide, voice is our means, and courage is our companion.

The Awakening

A few years ago, I came upon a thought-provoking quote: "When even one person is oppressed, none of us is free." It had such significance for me that I tacked it on a bulletin board over my desk.

A few months later, within a three-week period, five women were murdered in Minnesota in acts of domestic violence. One was stabbed sixteen times in the chest and stomach. I felt sick, sad, and angry. A little bit of my own psyche died along with those women, and I felt powerless to do anything about it. The quote on my bulletin board was revealing the truth to my body and my soul.

A friend called me the next week and said that several writers and artists wanted to do something to protest the violence. She wondered if I would be interested in participating.

I had to ponder this invitation, because it tapped into a residual panic at facing anything involving rage, violence, and danger. Her invitation took me on an inward journey through the past few years, when

I had left a lucrative professional partnership after recognizing the severe emotional abuse I sustained there. I was seeing a counselor and a spiritual director to unravel the repercussions of that episode.

I knew that my childhood was somehow involved in this pain, and I began remembering recurring episodes at our kitchen table in which I heard my mother cry and my father rage, while I was too afraid to move. I remembered a poem I had eked out during a love relationship in which I was—although I was not yet fully conscious of it—emotionally and sexually abused. I only knew at the time that I must and would survive, and the poem gave voice to that deeply felt need.

> You say
> *I love you*
> and put your hands
> around my neck
> squeeze and laugh
> scratch my back
> until it screams
>
> In me grows
> a very small NO
> in the center
> of my soul
> from the place
> of deepest knowing
>
> Passion is what we
> need in our lives
> you say
> The scabs
> on my breasts
> keep me awake
> all night long
>
> Months go by
> I nourish NO
> I feed it
> mother's milk
>
> You are always so kind
> when the pain is over
> So kind I wonder
> if it really is
> just my imagination
> just me going crazy

I nurse the NO with
every last ounce
of energy I have
At times I think
it must have died without
sucking or writhing
only murmurs
fighting death

You laugh
when I say
I'm scared
You spray spit
in my face and
take me by the hand
to go for a walk
There's no reason
to be afraid
you say

The NO grows
It begins to crawl
to walk
to look around
the NO has
no right
to speak

Finally it whispers
its first words
stop
hurting me

Your fury
breaks forth

But the NO
does not die
It knows it
has a right
It grows
and speaks

At last the NO
loosens it bonds

I say NO
and for the first time
I know I will never die

I decided to say yes to my friend's invitation, and we started meeting with other women writers, artists, and activists to plan what we could do. Out of these meetings came the idea for an exhibit of life-sized, red, wooden figures representing the twenty-seven women who had been killed in Minnesota in one year. Each figure would include a heart-shaped shield on its chest, telling the woman's story. It came to be called the Silent Witness Exhibit. We worked with several women's organizations to raise the money and produce the exhibit.

The exhibit's opening was planned to coincide with an annual event, Women Come to the Capitol, when women from all over the state come to meet legislators and learn lobbying techniques. Our plan was to have 500 women march the figures from a church to the capitol rotunda for a press conference. I was excited and scared about the opening.

On the morning of the march, I woke up with such severe pain in my side and back that I could not move. I had never experienced this before and had no idea what was wrong. I just knew I was petrified and I couldn't move. The pain slowly dissipated and my husband took me to the emergency room of a local hospital when I was able to walk. All morning we waited to find out what was wrong. No one knew. They narrowed it down to gall stones or muscle spasms. I left the hospital weak and shaken and got to the church just in time for the march, having missed the morning's proceedings. The march was wonderful, but I was a mess. I didn't know what was wrong and I still felt scared.

As usual, I went to the sources of my strength in times of trouble: my journal and my spirituality. I knew there was a message in here somewhere, but I was hard pressed to find it. This is an excerpt from my journal.

> "I am so confused. I thought I was supposed to do this project and now my body is rebelling, stopping me. I wish I knew what this was all about. Should I stop working on this? Please show me the way and help me listen to what my body is telling me."

The breakthrough came when I worked publicly against domestic violence a second time and felt the pain again. I became certain that these were muscle spasms and that they were directly related to the debut of the Silent Witness Exhibit. The spasms were my body's way of warning me that I was breaking family rules by speaking out against abuse. I was in awe of the power of the rules and also of the power of my body to carry the warning so effectively. What an amazing discovery. It was like being on sacred ground, even though the implications were frightening. Would this happen every time I spoke out? Would I have to stop my involvement?

I met with my professional and personal support system: my counselor, my doctor, my spiritual director, my masseuse, and the friends I worked with on the Silent Witness Exhibit. I decided on a course of action that included honoring my body and taking care of it, writing about the experience, talking to my body before I went out again, and taking a couple of ibuprofen tablets to help relax my muscles. I got twinges for a year after the initial event but never another full-blown attack.

The Abyss

That spasm triggered some deep personal issues and threw me into a dark personal abyss, whose walls stretched up for miles from the dark pit in which I sat for months, not able to move internally or make any sense of the night. I saw no guides who could help me, no light at the top of the abyss.

The only sound I could imagine was the flapping of wings, which I concluded were bats fluttering around me. It was frightening, but at least I didn't feel totally alone. I wrote faithfully in my journal and found solace in one writer, T. S. Eliot. Here is the poem I held close to my heart during those months of darkness.

> I said to my soul, be still, and wait without hope
> For hope would be hope for the wrong thing; wait without love
> For love would be love of the wrong thing; there is yet faith
> But the faith and the love and the hope are all in the waiting,
> Wait without thought, for you are not ready for thought:
> So the darkness shall be the light, and the stillness the dancing.
> —FOUR QUARTETS, "EAST COKER"

The source of the darkness was my inability to acknowledge the frightening truth of my life. As that truth slowly emerged, I knew it had the power to heal or destroy. The truth was that I was a smart, successful woman who was also a victim of abuse. I had not learned how to take responsibility for my own safety and happiness. I was feeling powerless. The still more sobering truth was that I was in an emotionally abusive marriage and I had to decide what I was willing to do to change that, since, although I was not responsible for the abuse, I could not expect someone else to change it for me.

The desert became a strong metaphor for me. In my journal I wrote:

"I am distressed. This is a desert experience and the oases are hard to find. This feels long and fruitless, a waiting, holding-on-to-me-for-safety time. No water, no nourishment. I feel dry and wasted. I feel dormant."

During that time, I was taking drawing classes, something I had not done for fifteen years. I went to see my drawing teacher after class one day to tell her I couldn't draw anymore. She asked why. I told her I was in too deep a personal abyss. She looked at me compassionately and said, "Just draw what you see on the walls of the abyss."

"Right," I said. "I don't see anything on the walls of the abyss."

She paused for a moment and said, "Just wait for a while. You will."

I went home discouraged, wanting to withdraw from the world, as any true introvert in personal crisis would. But I stayed with my spiritual discipline of praying, recording dreams, and writing in my journal every morning as if someone was listening, even though I wondered if that were so. And I kept moving slowly through the routines of my life. A few weeks later, I was reading Joseph Campbell's *The Power of Myth*. I turned a page and saw a drawing that grabbed my psyche almost violently, it was so powerful.

The drawing was of Kali, the Hindu goddess of death and fertility, in the middle of a ritual in which she killed four generals with one plunge of her ferocious pitchfork. Around her neck and hanging from each ear she wore a matched set of jewelry made of the shrunken bodies of previous victims, and from her mouth emerged a snake-like tongue that twisted to find its prey.

She had me. Intellectually, I hated the violence of the painting, but I knew emotionally that it was what I had to embrace. I had to wrestle with Kali, with her rage. She was my angel, and if I did not wrestle with her I would not receive the most profound gift of my life, my own freedom. So for the next three months, in all my spare time, I drew every detail of Kali in her rage. I even drew close-up inserts of the parts of her that were especially gruesome—her necklace, her tongue, her tiger-head leg covering, the pitchfork entering the generals.

Then I had a mind-boggling dream. Dreams are spiritual messages that you are being lovingly cared for by divine forces. They are like angels, in that they bring both good news and urgent warnings. My dream was an urgent warning. In the dream, I was alone and locked in a burning box car on a short train, which was traveling on a track shaped like a figure eight, the symbol for infinity. On the outside of the burning car was a plaque with my mother's name on it.

I knew instantly that this was a warning dream and that I must make some changes or this would be my fate. I worked with my professional support team and made several decisions. One was to put my marriage on the line to stop the abusive cycle. That felt like the most courageous act of my life. At the same time, I decided to coordinate the Silent Witness Exhibit and start speaking more publicly about domestic violence. I started writing again, and letting my writing help me to the next place, although I could not see where I was headed. Once I made these important decisions, my writing angel startled me by taking me in a new direction.

Kali, along with my journal and nightly vivid dreams, took me on a spiritual journey I had never imagined could be considered normal or healing. They took me to my rage, my ocean of energy, which had been repressed every time I was abused. My rage at three bosses who sexually harassed me in my twenties; my rage at living in fear at home, at years of marriage in passive-aggressive and openly abusive systems. Rage, rage, rage. My journal bulged with the emotion. Just listen:

> "My rage at this violence goes so deep I can feel it in my leg muscles, my back, my arms, my feet. It is a very bleak time. This has got to stop. I am very frightened and exceptionally angry—crystal clear anger, totally undiluted—and holy fear. I don't know whether to give up or go on. Show me the way. Show me the way. What is the way out?"

The effect was miraculous. My anger began to move into raw energy that needed to be managed lest it spiral out of control. I channeled it into writing and into setting boundaries in my marriage, to change the system we had so elaborately and unknowingly built. My husband sought healing for himself, and we both started moving into new territory in our relationship. It was the most difficult, courageous, and life-giving decision we have ever made.

My writing took a surprising turn. Story became much more important to me, because I began honoring my own story. I wrote a murder mystery, using my shadow side to create the perpetrator. That took me into an entirely new writing landscape, which was opened to me by my stay with the darkness. I ventured into the world of fantasy by writing a story about a star that goes on a journey to find its soul by facing the dark. The star turned out to be the Bethlehem star.

At that point, I thought I had seen enough pain and turmoil and was ready to get back to my normal work life. I was wrong. Maybe I could see my core, but I had not yet become intimate with it. Another event changed all that.

My best male friend and my co-author on a spiritual development book died unexpectedly from a heart attack at the age of fifty-two. I was in Eastern Europe and friends couldn't make contact with me until the funeral was over. In the numbness that followed, I tried to sort out how I could go on. I thought I would never write again. As a healing experience, I tried to draw my friend's face but had more trouble each time I tried. One day, in the middle of that struggle, I looked at his picture on my desk and heard him say, "Stop trying to draw me, Janet. Write for both of us."

The courage to face my loss, and to face the fear at my core, released me to write and teach more courageously. I began moving into overtly spiritual topics in my writing classes, and changes started happening in my students' writing. After I started coordinating the Silent Witness Exhibit and watched it travel around the state, I felt compelled to write the story of the exhibit for other people to hear and replicate. It culminated in a book, *The Silent Witness Story*, which is now in its second printing.

Light was beginning to pierce through the darkness; the stillness was dancing. T. S. Eliot was right. I was beginning to think the light was worth waiting for. This freedom was energizing me. I felt my soul, and I felt compassion, and I was unafraid for the first time in my life. My marriage was healing in a slow and profound way. Emotional intimacy looked like a real possibility, and I began learning about love for the first time. The light even became bright enough to see that the sound of flapping wings, which I had thought was made by bats, was really the sound of angels. Tears of release and gratefulness flooded through me.

I had tapped into my core and there I found my passion. Passion to write on difficult topics, take on unpopular issues, delve into forms I had not tried before. I started writing articles on the spirituality of the writing process for a literary magazine. I rewrote a book on power I had written ten years previously and put in a new chapter on leading from your soul. After two years of searching for a new publisher, it found a home and it found its voice in the world in a new way. I wrote humor and radio commentaries, and my teaching moved to deeper levels. As a public speaker, I was telling more of my story and taking more risks with the content of my talks. In my role as spiritual director, I was able to stay with people's pain, so that they knew they were not alone or abandoned.

Another miracle occurred without my noticing at first. The wife of our newly elected senator was interested in the issue of domestic violence and saw the Silent Witness Exhibit. She was drawn to it and asked us if there was any way we could bring it to Washington, D.C., to help effect legislation. This was more than any of us on the organizing committee expected, even though one of our stated goals was to march figures from all fifty states down Pennsylvania Avenue some day. We raised the money and six months later the Silent Witness Exhibit stood in the rotunda of the Russell Senate Office Building.

On opening night, several senators saw the exhibit and many people told us they were very moved by the stories of our twenty-seven women—women who had been mothers, wives, sisters, and employees just a few short years ago. Telling my story at the opening event was one of the most moving moments of my life. That week, legislation on child safety centers was introduced and hearings were held on the bill, which passed out of committee unopposed two weeks later and became part of the larger Crime Bill. We believe the Witnesses had something to do with that. After that week in Washington, I believed I had done what I was put on earth to do: End the abuse in my own life and bring national attention to the violence in our country.

I've become a believer. A believer in the spiritual process and in the presence of angels. I am willing to let my writing take me to new places, and to trust the Holy to do the right thing in me. I think I can capture this experience in one sentence: "On the wings I acquired through suffering, I will soar (Mahler)." This does not mean that my life has become easy, stress-free, or painless. But it does mean that I can find peace in the middle of the chaos and a path through the pain. I have an inner well from which to gain strength and power.

In *Care of The Soul,* Thomas Moore says,

> "If we want to live from our depths—soulfully—then we will have to give up all pretenses to innocence as the shadow grows darker. The chief reward of surrendering innocence, so that the soul may be fully expressed, is an increase of power. In the presence of deep power, life becomes robust and passionate, signs that the soul is engaged and being given expression."

I am reminded again and again of the quote over my desk (now surrounded by statues of angels) that got all of this started. When even one person is oppressed, none of us is free. I am now less oppressed. And I believe in my soul that when I am less oppressed, everyone else is more free.

Reflecting on the Chapter

1. Have you had an awakening event in your life? What was it?

2. Has darkness ever become light for you?

3. Tell your story of moving from the darkness to the light in poetry, memoir, short story, or essay form.

4. How has your writing changed as a result of your experience?

Writing Exercises

1. What is your most memorable writing experience?

2. What is your scariest writing experience?

3. What are you afraid to have others know about you?

4. Write a statement or choose a poem, piece of scripture, or quote to guide you through difficult times.

Visual Exercise

See your personal story as a TV program. Choose the title, the type of show, the advertisers, and the stars. Sketch the plot and project the ending. Then watch the program in your imagination. How does it affect you?

Guided Imagery

Go to that quiet place in the center of yourself and be gently there alone for a few minutes. This is a sacred and safe place, a place in which the Holy can speak to you. Let your imagination show you a large wall in front of you on which words sometimes appear. Do you see any words now? What are they? What meaning do they have for you? Ask the Holy to show you the special words that will be your guidelines as you write and tell your story. Look at the wall to see what the words are. What meaning do they have for you? Thank the Holy and return to the room you are in. Write about the words and the Holy in your journal.

FOUR

Honoring Nurture and Discipline

> "Inspiration and genius are not everything. While Mozart composed, the phone didn't ring."
> —*ANONYMOUS*

This quote was given to me on a card by one of my students. I laughed out loud and then I thought about it again. It carried a truth that illustrates a central paradox in writing: that nurture and discipline, though seemingly at odds with one another, are both necessary in the writing process.

Nurturing ourselves as writers is useful and supportive. Nurture can include self-care, positive self-talk, angel presences, imagery, and the like. I have found, though, that nurture alone, without self-appraisal and discipline, causes many writers to become stuck in the process of writing and never get to their goals.

On the other hand, discipline helps writers produce and complete work, and make it public. Discipline can include time schedules, goals, the effective use of the critic, attention to craft, and self-analysis. Yet discipline alone can produce driven and callused writers.

So the issue is, how do we balance nurture and discipline so we can give ourselves what is lacking at any given time. Sometimes I need to heal from a painful writing experience, but eventually I have to get up and try again or I may quit writing. Sometimes, when I have been writing too much, I need to get away from it and simply *be* for a while. My writing, when I come back to it, will be better.

Nurture

When distilled, nurture is essentially two things: belief in oneself and care for oneself. There are many different ways to develop these aspects of ourselves as part of a spiritual process in which we let the Holy teach us about love and caring, but there are also concrete ways to remind ourselves of the spiritual process at work inside. I will mention five of these; they are ways that my students and I have used.

Visual reminders

Using visual images (pictures, symbols, figures, posters, sayings, the view out the window) in the place where you write is a personal and powerful way to remind yourself that this is a sacred space, that you are called to write here, and that you can have the courage to do that. My computer desk is surrounded now by six (at last count) angels, a photo, twelve stuffed animals, a mouse puppet, lots of books, a tea pot, my cat, and a compact disc player—just for starters. It's not neat but it is definitely my space, and it sets me in the mood to write even before I sit down.

Quotes from other writers; reading other writers

It can be inspiring to read other writers (unless you have an overactive critic). Reading is a way many writers nurture themselves. At the very least, you can pick up craft ideas or content nuances.

You may find it helpful to jot down quotes about the writing process. On the bad days, it helps to know that other writers have already been through these days and survived. These are some of my favorites:

"Nobody can counsel and help you, nobody. There is only one single way. Go into yourself. Search for the reason that bids you to write; find out whether it is spreading out its roots in the deepest places of your heart, acknowledge to yourself whether you would have to die if it were denied you to write. This above all—ask yourself in the stillest hour of your night: Must I write?"

"Be patient toward all that is unsolved in your heart and try to love the questions themselves like locked rooms and like books that are written in a very foreign tongue. Do not now seek the answers, which cannot be given you because you would not be able to live them. And the point is, to live everything. Live the questions now. Perhaps you will then gradually, without noticing it, live along some distant day into the answer."

—Rainer Maria Rilke, *Letters to a Young Poet*

"Never be afraid. *Never*. Only be courageous."

"Everybody is talented, original, and has something important to say."

"No writing is a waste of time."

"Writing, the creative effort, the use of the imagination, should come first,—at least for some part of every day of your life. It is a wonderful blessing if you will use it. You will become happier, more enlightened, alive, impassioned, light-hearted and generous to everybody else. Even your health will improve. Colds will disappear and all the other ailments of discouragement and boredom. And that is why I have come to think that the only way to become a better writer is to become a better person."

—Brenda Ueland, *If You Want to Write*; personal interview

"Feed the lake. All writers feed the lake. Some are rivers (Tolstoy), others trickles. Just feed the lake."

—Jean Rhys, as quoted in *The Writer*

"We cannot be mature artists if we have lost the ability to believe which we had as children. An artist at work is in a condition of complete and total faith."

"Giving birth to a baby or a story is ultimately mystery."

"When a shoddy novel is published the writer is rejecting the obedient response, taking the easy way out. But when the words mean even more than the writer knew they meant, then the writer has been listening."

"The artist cannot hold back; it is impossible, because writing, or any other discipline of art, involves participation in suffering, in the ills and the occasional stabbing joys that come from being part of the human drama"

—Madeleine L'Engle, *Walking on Water*

"In your natural way of producing words, there is a sound, a texture, a rhythm—voice—which is the main source of power in your writing. It's the only voice you've got."

—Peter Elbow, *Writing Without Teachers*

"If I found out I had only ten minutes left to live, I'd just type faster."
—Isaac Asimov

Enter into writing in a sacred way

Each time you sit down to write, think about entering into a sacred space in which you are surrounded with support. Writers do that in various ways. One way is to summon a brief image in your mind of what makes this space and time sacred for you. That image may be of a mentor, the Holy one, the light, a sense of calling. Let yourself be in that space while breathing slowly, until you have settled into the mood of writing. Ask what you need to write today and listen carefully for the answer.

Follow it, even if it takes you in a new direction.

Some writers use rituals to begin their writing. A candle lit near your writing space acts as a constant reminder that you are in the presence of light. Some writers play a certain kind of music in the background, others wear certain clothes or hats. The important thing is that the ritual matter to you, that it be meaningful and not something you think you ought to do because someone else does it. If rituals don't work for you, don't do them.

Another way to begin writing is to pray into the experience by asking the Holy to guide you in your writing and take you to the places your writing bids you. Some people write a prayer and use it every time they write. Others pray whatever is in their hearts at the moment.

A student, Christine, wrote her own prayer, using an opening sentence from a Native American Prayer in Edward Hays' *Prayers of a Planetary Pilgrim.*

O Great Spirit
whose voice I hear in the wind,
and whose breath gives life to all the earth,
hear me.
Open me to your will, your grace and your gifts,
Lead me to the peace of your spirit and
the strength of your soul.
I now allow all that is mine by divine right
to be released into the world.

A friend, Jill Breckenridge, wrote this prayer for her creative work:

At this moment and for all eternity, I offer you my heart, mind, body, and spirit, dedicating to you whatever work you would do through me.

Help me be unerringly true to the inner voice—let it surprise me with truths I didn't know I knew. Help me let go of the ground of rigid rationality for the sake of the creative, intuitive leap. As my creative genius is released, help me to set aside my little ego and be obedient to the risk and to the work.

May I live a constant prayer, and may faith in your plan for me defeat all fear in the knowledge that my task is merely to do the work at hand. Let my faith be supported by patience, since patience accompanies all deep love. During times when the work is difficult, let me know you will never give me a job for which I am not prepared.

Hone the edge of my discipline so that I may cut through any resistance, remembering that a disciple is one who is allured and attracted to her work. Let me be brave enough to forge the creative fire which turns that which is old into the new.

Let me die to self and live inspired in the work I have been given to do, knowing that for now and for all time, all shall be well, and all shall be well, and all manner of things shall be well. Thy will be done. Amen.

Many of the world's holy books speak of writing. Some writers like to go to these ancient texts and experience the affirmation they gave to writers thousands of years ago. Here are two texts from the book of Isaiah, in the Bible, which refer to words and writing.

The Lord God has given me
The tongue of those who are taught,
that I may know how to sustain with a word
those that are weary

Morning by morning God wakens my ear,
God wakens my ear
to hear as those who are taught.
The Lord God has opened my ear,
and I was not rebellious,
I turned not backward.
    ISAIAH 50:4,5

And I have put my words in your mouth,
and hid you in the shadow of my hand,
Stretching out the heavens

and laying the foundations of the earth,
and saying to Zion, "You are my people."
    ISAIAH 51:16

Creating a safe, nurturing environment

This can include things as simple as a comfortable chair in which to write or type, a desk that is a special writing space, or privacy. While these may seem simple, choosing them may be a statement of confidence in your writing. Virginia Woolf talked about having a room of one's own. Writers need a space that is their own, where they can leave their writing files and keep their notes, pens, or disks.

For some writers, this space includes the right pen and paper, the right lighting or music, the right tea or a favorite pet. It doesn't matter what it is, as long as the environment is conducive to writing.

Environment can also mean more than the immediate space in which you write. It can include times of the year and parts of the country in which you prefer to write. Some writers work best when they go on extended writing retreats, where the daily necessities are taken care of for them. One of my friends spends three or four days at a time at a hotel to meet book deadlines. She writes best in a marathon style. There is so much going on in her life that if she doesn't get away from it, the distractions keep her from writing.

Support

Support accompanies both nurturing and discipline. Support for nurturing is available in the form of journal writing, talking to friends who are supportive of writing, walking in nature, or being with friends who ask you how your writing is going (and care what your answer is). It is important to distinguish supportive people from poisonous people. Supportive people give you encouragement even when they give you criticism. They do not cripple your spirit. Poisonous people, no matter how helpful they intend to be, stifle or discourage you. People can know you well and be fine writers themselves, yet still not be supportive for you. It is crucial to your writing and your soul to find support.

Discipline

The other half of the equation is discipline. The essence of discipline is seeing writing as part of the core of who we are and treating it as a calling. This will encourage us to do the tasks and take the risks that discipline requires of us. What are the elements of discipline?

Time

Many writers say time is what keeps them from being as productive as they'd like. Yet writers who don't write at all have the same number of hours in the week as those who write one evening a week, one day a week, or five days a week. How we choose to use our time depends on both our circumstances (children, jobs, volunteer activities, income) and our attitude towards ourselves and our writing. Every writer has to make the decision to start writing.

There are rhythms to writing. Some writers go through quiet times, or silent periods, as Tillie Olson called them in *Silences*. These are times when the pen is silent but things are going on inside, even if the writer may be largely unaware of them. The silence may last for months or for years, and there will be times when the writer wonders if she will ever write again and longs for that first yearning that turns into actual writing.

Some writers write best early in the morning, others late at night. Some can write in ten-minute bursts, others need two-hour blocks. I know writers who drop snippets of paper into wallets or purses and use them later, and others who keep files of chapter details they've been collecting for years. Speed writing in notebooks works for some writers, while others outline books in their heads. The chapter on learning styles will give you a better understanding of why this is true.

Goals

For many writers, having goals works well. These can be self-imposed or externally imposed. Setting a goal starts you into a mode of being in which you are productive and keep yourself on track, so the parts of the writing process that you do not like don't loom as large. You know they're just part of the process, and you'll be able to do your favorite part soon.

Before I imagined this book you are reading, my goal was to write—in addition to my other work—two essays a year for the literary magazine in which its earliest portions appeared. It did not occur to me these essays could become a book until I had written three of them and the editor mentioned the idea to me.

Another writer I know loves to write humorous and philosophical articles about fishing. Fishing magazines do not accept many of these, but he likes them and keeps stockpiling them. I have a feeling that someday they will become a book, since he already has written two serious books about fishing and is seen as a local expert. In his spare time, he is a professor of philosophy at a local college.

I believe it helps to write down our long-range goals. I think we become more serious about them and they slip into our subconscious mind, where we can nurture them. Once, in my mid-twenties, when I was making my first job change, I wrote down a list of all my options in four different categories: realities, possibilities, drudgeries, and fantasies. Realities were what I was qualified for, possibilities were a mild stretch, drudgeries were what I could do if I was starving, and fantasies were what I wanted to do before I died. I lost the list somewhere and found it six years later, when I moved. I was doing two of my fantasies, running a business and writing a book. Once those ideas got into my subconscious, they became more real to me and I unconsciously moved in those directions.

Taking risks

I ask students in my classes to take a risk, whatever that means for them. It's a good way to find out what we're afraid of in writing, what gets in our way. I surveyed several classes some time ago to find out what got in the way for my students. By far the greatest obstacle was fear—fear of success, fear they were no good, fear of what would come out or what they would learn if they wrote. The second greatest obstacle was not believing in themselves, not having the confidence to speak, not having anything to say. The third was lack of time, the fourth was not being clear what they were writing about, and the fifth, sixth, and seventh were fatigue, housework, and perfectionism.

Taking a risk means facing those things you are afraid of and moving slowly into the dark space they occupy. There is no other way to make progress in the writing process. And the shadows are never quite as dark as they appear. The surprise is that in the back of the shadow, where you can barely see it, is the surprise, the truth, the genius, the gift.

Another way to take a risk in writing is to make your work more public: by reading in front of people, giving your writing as gifts, or sending things out for publication. Each time you cross another barrier, you learn more about yourself, and your writing is affected positively in the long run.

Craft

For many writers, discipline consists of learning the craft of writing, the techniques peculiar to each form or genre. That may range from metaphor or form in poetry to methods of criticism in literature, from scientific inquiry in science fiction to facts about food in cook books.

Many writing classes deal with craft, and learning about it is a good way to increase our confidence. Classes on craft can link us with other writers with whom we can talk, network, or exchange ideas. Going to a class or writers' support group regularly strengthens our discipline, even if we are not writing all the time. It gets us thinking about writing.

Challenges from other writers

Relationships with other writers can be an important discipline. They can support and push us because they know us and our writing strengths as well as our foibles. They are not jealous of us or trying to compete. They are there to help us become what we dream of being. They are invaluable, because we can trust them and they will help us get over our biggest hurdles, the hurdles we think no one else understands.

One of my most ardent writing buddies was there for me when a book of mine was out of print and I had put it aside, assuming it was dead. She was not ready to accept that, because she believed in the book and knew I did too, even though I was discouraged. At lunch one day, she suggested that I send my book to a publisher who specialized in out-of-print books. I waited a while and then cautiously followed her suggestion. The book was republished by that publisher and is doing well. My friend was an angel for me, just when I needed to have one.

Gifts of the spiritual process

Many gifts emerge on the spiritual journey of writing, as a result of honoring both nurture and discipline. We hear and honor our own voice, even if it is different from other people's voices; we gain courage to write what we are compelled to write; we become willing to engage with our critic and our angel, our shadow and our fears; we have insights from our inner wisdom and from the Holy through dreams and images; and we experience our writing as a calling. I write about these gifts in detail in other chapters.

Right now, I would like to start you thinking about what the spiritual process looks and feels like when you're in the middle of the writing life. The following are a few clues that a spiritual process is at work in your writing. You will find many more for yourself.

- Being afraid or embarrassed to write, but still writing.
- Finding that letters to friends and family seem to write themselves.
- Sitting still when no writing comes and allowing yourself to listen.
- Remembering painful events or memories that elicit writing.
- Honoring times of day that most nurture memories and creative thoughts.
- Learning to listen to your writing.
- Observing poems that pop up and want to have a voice.
- Observing that things you write after long walks, fresh air, or prayer are more compelling, more inspired.
- Being willing to obey the Holy in your writing process.
- Processing dreams that want to be remembered.
- Allowing journal insights to stay with you and guide you.
- Seeing that non-writing times serve a purpose in your life.
- Acknowledging your angels.
- Observing a strong pull or push from within you to write.
- Receiving writing topics out of nowhere.
- Watching characters take over a story.
- Staying with a story, book, or peom for years if necessary.

- Writing about worrying about writing, but without worrying.
- Honoring current life and world events that seek reflection within you.
- Observing nagging thoughts and insights that want to be public.
- Struggling with unanswerable questions.
- Being willing to change topics if you are called to do so.
- Being willing to face your fear of writing.
- Meeting publishers, agents, or editors who like their work and do it as a labor of love.
- Collaborating with others as a nourishing experience.
- Having the courage to write on difficult topics, in new forms, or with your own authentic voice.
- Approaching writing with a prayer and sense of the sacred.
- Experiencing loss of ego attachment to the work.
- Being willing to write what is given to you by the Holy.
- Praising and enjoying other people's work without diminishing your own.
- Being willing to risk whatever it takes to write.
- Wanting to heal childhood wounds.
- Being willing to write with integrity.
- Writing from your soul.

Reflecting on the Chapter

1. What is the best way for you to nurture yourself as a writer?

2. What issues emerge when you try to nurture yourself?

3. What is your best discipline as a writer?

4. What issues emerge when you try to discipline yourself?

5. What are the clues that spirituality is at work in your writing?

Writing Exercises

1. The quote or affirmation I need for myself is ...

2. My favorite writer is …
   Because …

3. When I have both nurture and discipline, my writing is …

4. The thing I most long for in my writing is …

Visual Exercise

Draw symbols or a picture that represents both nurture and discipline for you.

Guided Imagery

Imagine yourself in a room, half of which is devoted to support and nurture and the other half to discipline. What do the two halves of the room look like? What colors are they, what textures, what temperatures? Which side of the room are you most drawn to? Try taking the things you like from each side of the room and moving them to your own room, to assist you in your writing. What is that like? How is it different from the way you write now? Write about that in your journal.

FIVE

The Writer's Wheel: Spokes

Each time I begin a new writing class, I ask the participants, "What is your name? Why are you taking this class? What do you read?" They are eager and articulate in answering the first two questions, but embarrassed or reticent about what they read. I hear comments like, "Well, I just read for enjoyment," or, "I'm reading memoir, but I could never write that way," or, "I have to confess to reading escape and self-help stuff." Reluctantly and apologetically, they talk about what they read.

After they finish describing their reading habits, I tell them that my experience suggests they will write best in the form they read the most, especially if they are new at writing. Groans, smiles of recognition, looks of fear, and sighs of relief all emerge at that juncture.

But I do have their attention.

The underlying assumption I hear from them is either that what they are reading is not "good" literature, or that what they are reading is too good and too well written for them to ever aspire to it.

Both assumptions are irrelevant in the writing process.

I developed the Writer's Wheel in order to minimize assumptions that soon become writing blocks. It describes the four ingredients necessary to the writing process, then combines these ingredients in various ways to make up all six of the writing forms. This helps writers understand their strengths and describes what they need to do if they want to stretch themselves.

I believe there are two major ways to produce great writing, and I offer them for your consideration. One way is to use all four of the spokes in the wheel. That takes practice and self-knowledge. You build up to it as you gain appreciation, experience, and confidence. The other way is to take the inward spiritual journey to your core, embracing your critic and wrestling with your angel, a process I describe in Section Three: Letting Your Writing Take You Deeper. The ultimate writing experience might be to do both.

In this first chapter on the Writer's Wheel, I will describe the four ingredients of writing. In the next chapter, I will explain how these four create all six writing forms. I am deliberately taking the writing process apart to show how we can choose forms that will encourage our natural strengths and help us become great writers instead of choosing forms that make writing harder.

Many of us choose our writing forms without being fully conscious of it. That is fine as long as we are not sabotaging ourselves. The Writer's Wheel brings these choices to consciousness and helps us accept our strengths as a gift. If you have found your preferred learning style, you may notice a correlation with the four ingredients in the writer's wheel. If you are enthusiastic, you may be drawn to spirit; if imaginative, to technique; if logical, to structure; and if practical, to content.

The Writer's Wheel: The Four Ingredients as Spokes

The Writer's Wheel has four spokes, *all useful and all equal.* Each spoke represents one of the four ingredients of the writing process. Writers do their best by entering the wheel, or writing process, wherever they have energy, talent, or interest. If you are naturally drawn to character development or dialogue, the technique spoke is your most comfortable place to enter; if you love research, facts, and structure, you'll be drawn to the structure spoke; if you like ideas and want to affect people's thinking, you will gravitate to the content spoke; if you resonate to life experience and feeling content you'll like the spirit spoke; if writers choose to add a spoke or move to another spoke because they are curious or like a challenge, they can. Since all the spokes are equal, the move to a new spoke, or the addition of a spoke, results in growth.

Four Spokes and the Writing Process

The four ingredients of the writing process, which are represented by the spokes, are: spirit, which asks why; technique, which asks how;

Figure 8

structure, which asks when, where, and in what framework; and content, which asks what and toward what end. Let me explain each of these spokes and describe the central issues for each group.

Spirit

The spirit spoke involves the source or energy of writing. It asks us why we are writing, and with what inner connection. Spirit describes our motivation, drive, and source of energy to write. What is it that fuels our fire and makes us sit down, again and again, to write?

Our muse, angel, and, yes, our critic are all ingredients in this spirit factor. How do we see ourselves as writers? What is our soul trying to form in us? How are we personally involved with our writing? Where is our writing taking us? And what kind of support do we need from ourselves and others to write our best? What is our voice and how do we find it? How do we know it is ours and not someone else's? What is our passion?

If there is no spirit or energy, we may write technically proficient pieces, but they will have a flatness that readers will notice. Spirit is the spoke that takes the most courage to develop and requires an inner spiritual journey. In my experience, the spirit spoke is the most neglected ingredient in the writing process, and the most elusive to teach.

The spirit spoke challenges us to honestly embrace ourselves as writers and find our authentic voice. This involves waiting, being silent, letting our writing take us to places we've never been before, letting ourselves be great writers on a sacred journey.

As an example, a student of mine wrote well and had as her trademark a sarcastic, often venomous voice. She complained that her writing was in a rut and I asked her what the rut looked like. She said it was fiery and fierce. I asked her to write to the fiery fierceness. Her eyes squinted and a shot of anger clenched her face. I wondered whether she wanted to hold onto the anger for safety or whether she would let it go. I told her it would be a big challenge and might result in a breakthrough. She liked challenges. She went home and skipped the next class.

When she came back, she'd started writing to her fierceness and felt an eruption inside that she'd never experienced before. Something had let loose, and it felt like anger hitting her in the stomach with its fist. She wrote fast and furiously and the anger wrote back in large scraggly letters. It scared her, but she was willing to keep writing because she knew the anger held some secret she needed to know. Her anger had been helpful to her in the past, but had outlived its usefulness in her writing. Now it was blocking her passion. She faced it, and it gave her energy to write past the anger into her passion for music.

An example of spirit in writing comes from *Wisdomkeepers,* by Steve Wall and Harvey Arden. In it, Matthew King, a spokesman for the Lakota people, says, "When we want wisdom, we go up on the hill and talk to God. Four days and four nights, without food and water. Yes, you can talk to God up on a hill by yourself. You can say anything you want ... That's between you and God and nobody else. It's a great feeling to be talking to God. I know. I did it way up on the mountain. The wind was blowing. It was dark. It was cold. And I stood there and I talked to God."

Matthew King has spirit. He's bold. He's authentic. He talks to God.

Technique

Technique asks how. It's concerned with the method or craft of writing. It helps us select our particular slant on a piece of writing. It involves choosing the best and most interesting form for this particular piece. It includes our choice of words and phrases and our attention to the inner life of our writing.

Specific techniques include descriptive details, dialogue, characterization, use of metaphor, use of examples and illustrations, charts, graphs, stories, visuals, images, symbols. These are the material of most writing classes, and writing which neglects these skills entirely lacks vividness and breadth.

The technique spoke challenges us to follow the form in which our piece best fits, to experiment with new forms and techniques that tug at us, to break the rules, and to believe in our own approach, even if others are not comfortable with it.

As an example, a student of mine wanted to write a memoir about his family but was holding back, not wanting to use their names or describe incidents involving living people. His fear of hurting people was keeping him from writing the story. We talked about other forms the memoir could take. He began to see how the form he'd chosen made an impossible demand—tell the truth but don't incriminate anyone. He began to fictionalize the story and found more freedom and fewer obstacles.

The fiction of Verlyn Klinkenborg is an example of studied technique. In this excerpt from *The Last Fine Time*, you can sense the impending storm in Buffalo, New York:

> If you were the last person buying gas on a night like this, you would look up at the streetlamp overhead as you waited for the tank to fill with unleaded. You would see beyond it a ceiling— not a sky—of utter opacity, as black as the pupil of an owl's eye, out of which falls a globe of swirling snow. You would look at that owl's pupil, and you would readily imagine that there was nothing behind it, no moon or stars illuminating the tops of the clouds the way the streetlamp illuminates the snow on the ground. Nothing. You would stare into that owl's pupil of a night, and you would be the first to blink.

Structure

The structure spoke asks when, where, and in what framework will we write? How can we find the time and place to make writing a greater part of our lives? Structure also carries the infrastructure of our piece, the skeleton, format, and internal organization, the depth and texture. We need it to plan rhyme schemes, repeated images, the layout of the page, the plot of the story, the titles of the chapters, the shape of the poem, the location of the flashbacks.

The editor in us loves this process side of writing. We fiddle lovingly with sentence structure and paragraph size, as well as grammar, punctuation, spelling, repeated metaphor. Without structure, the piece has no backbone, no direction, no flow, and less depth.

The structure spoke challenges us to be patient and trust the process, to allow inspiration to guide us and not tie up every loose end.

As an example, a poet I know was working on a poem she felt very strongly about. She told me she had been redrafting it for several weeks and it still didn't sing to her the way she wanted it to. It was written in six long stanzas. Among other questions, I asked her where the poem wanted to go. She said it wanted a different shape.

"So what shape does it want?" I asked. She saw in her mind two stanzas of the poem—a totally different shape and style than she was used to. That change led to a breakthrough in her poetry.

An example of taking structure, words, meaning seriously is this excerpt from Ogden Nash's "Very Like a Whale."

> One thing that literature would be greatly the better for
> Would be a more restricted employment by authors of simile and
>   metaphor,
> Authors of all races, be they Greeks, Romans, Teutons or Celts,
> Can't seem just to say that anything is the thing it is but have to go
>   out of their way to say that it is like something else.
> What does it mean when we are told
> That the Assyrian came down like a wolf on the fold?
> In the first place, George Gordon Byron had had enough
>   experience
> To know that it probably wasn't just one Assyrian, it was a *lot* of
>   Assyrians.
> However, as too many arguments are apt to induce apoplexy and
>   thus hinder longevity,
> We'll let it pass as one Assyrian for the sake of brevity ...

Content

The content spoke asks, What should we write about? To what end are we writing? It asks us to attend carefully to content and audience. It can include subtle or bold messages to illustrate or underscore motives, causes, problems, issues, concepts, ideas, needs, theories, feelings.

This content spoke also includes the practical side of writing: the public reading, publishing, distribution, promotion, and marketing of our work. The business side of writing, some people call it, but really it is the *public* side, whatever form that takes, from reading aloud in classes or to friends, to giving your writing as gifts, to formal publishing.

This spoke challenges us to allow ourselves to be led by our writing itself into the depth of its content. It challenges us to listen to the piece to see how it wants to be made public, and to allow time for that process and understand the public side in a new way.

As an example, I have found ways to let my writing be public without necessarily publishing it. I have a longstanding struggle with sadness and pain at Christmas time. A few years ago, my angel invited me to redeem Christmas by investing my creativity in writing about the season. This resulted in three pieces that I've given to my friends as gifts. I have decided not to formally publish them but to let them be public as holiday gifts.

An example of bold, content-driven writing is Riane Eisler's *The Chalice and the Blade*. She is openly persuading us and is not interested in metaphor or simile.

> "Of all life-forms on this planet, only we can plant and harvest fields, compose poetry and music, seek truth and justice, teach a child to read and write—or even laugh and cry. Because of our unique ability to imagine new realities and realize these through ever more advanced technologies, we are quite literally partners in our own evolution. And yet, this same wondrous species of ours now seems bent on putting an end not only to its own evolution but to that of most life on our globe, threatening our planet with ecological catastrophe or nuclear annihilation."

Using the Spokes in the Writing Process

To illustrate how use the Writer's Wheel, let's take a situation—three people are in a closed room having a loud quarrel—and look at how four writers, each specializing in one spoke of the wheel, would approach a description of what's going on.

Spirit

The spirit people will be personally connected with this event. They will know these people and be concerned about the outcome. What is the energy of this fight doing to each person? What effects will this have on their relationships? They will describe the energy of the event, the changing feelings, the fears, the passion, the challenge. They are concerned with authenticity, and as a result their dialogue is likely to put us inside a participant in the fight so we can feel the experience first hand. They will not be detached, and so we, too, become intimately involved.

Technique

People using this spoke will describe the room itself in detail and with metaphor, including color, texture, and the placement of the furnishings and windows. Then they will let us know about the characters— what they look like and who's wearing what—and vividly describe the anger that is present. And they will toss in little things like fragrances and the view from the window.

Structure

People using this spoke will let us know where this room is in relation to the rest of the building. Is the room in a house, a school, a hospital? Is there a name plate on the door (or a title to this chapter)? We will learn the significance of this particular room in the lives of these people. The room will appear again in the story for its symbolic value. We will learn who else is involved in this fight and why. Of course, they will write the story with correct punctuation and in full sentences.

Content

The content people will tell us what is going on among the characters—who is saying what to whom, who is fighting whom, and why. We will learn how these characters have been connected in the past, how this whole fight got started in the first place, and what the deep-seated issues are in this fight. We will get hints (foreshadowings) of what may happen next and we will be set up for the next scene. We also may get a sense of who the audience is for this story, and how it could be promoted.

Enhancing your writing

Each spoke represents a specialty, a preference, even a bias at times. Once you know yours, you'll understand why you are drawn (or not drawn) to books thick with description, or to books that move the plot along, or that focus on relationships, or on infrastructure and word-smithing. You'll understand the natural biases of reviewers. If they are drawn to detailed description, they will not be as interested in plot-driven books. If content is important to them, detail and description will be less crucial. New forms and experimentation will excite some reviewers but be distasteful to others.

How can you use these four ingredients to enhance or expand your writing? First, you need to understand and appreciate all four of the spokes, seeing how important each is to the writing process, even though you probably relate best to one or two. Acknowledging all four will help you to appreciate writers whose emphasis is different from yours.

Second, you need to honor the spoke you are naturally drawn to, the one you are good at. Try not to downplay, overplay, or demean its importance. It is yours. It is worth developing and sustaining. Most writers have problems with this. The spoke they're drawn to is either too good for them or not good enough. If they are technique driven, they think their content is shallow, or if they are oriented to structure and grammar, they think they lack passion—or think they don't need any passion. Either they try to be someone else or they refuse to grow.

In *Care of the Soul,* Thomas Moore describes this dilemma.

"Many of us spend time and energy trying to be something that we are not. But this is a move against soul, because individuality rises out of the soul as water rises out of the depths of the earth. . . . Power begins in knowing this special soul, which may be entirely different from our fantasies about who we are or who we want to be."

Stand back and observe what you are best at. Start there by asking the Holy to help you honor that as your gift. This is a profound experience and a key to the writing process. Then talk to your critic about how your spoke is the right one, the best one for you. That does not mean you won't ever need to branch out or develop further as a writer, but if you never honor your gift, you'll always be trying to hide it.

Third, add another spoke to your repertoire. A wheel rolls better with two spokes than with one. The added spoke can be any one of the other three, but you should choose the one that really interests you, not the one you *think* you should choose. Keep these two spokes in the back of your mind when you next write.

If you're best at writing with energy and feeling (spirit) in your journal and you are intrigued by technique, try fictionalizing your experiences, or adding dialogue to your writing. Or use metaphors to describe some aspect of the experience. You might already do this instinctively; so make it conscious.

Or let's say you're great at choosing the structure of a poem and using metaphors (structure). Try adding the content spoke by writing about provocative ideas.

If you're good at writing about other people's ideas or theories (content), experiment with a subject that brings up enormous energy or deeply felt emotions. You will be adding spirit to your facts.

When you have more experience and confidence, you can try using all four spokes. Start by adding one spoke, then add another when you are comfortable. This is the most balanced way of writing, but it is not the only way to reach the reader. Most people find they naturally write using two spokes.

To develop your writing style so that it includes all four spokes, you need to be conscious of what the spokes are. You need to let your writing take you to new places; it will enlarge you in the process. When a writer uses all four spokes naturally, I call this great or miraculous writing. I will come back to this in the next chapter.

Whenever you combine two spokes or ingredients of the Writer's Wheel, you are choosing one of the six forms of writing. The six forms are entertaining, inspirational, instructional, personal, persuasive, and fanciful. Most of us choose our form unconsciously, but that can lead us to be overly critical of ourselves, and to choose forms we think are too hard or not good enough. By being conscious of the form we choose, we can help ourselves become better writers.

In the next chapter I'll explain what the six writing forms are and how to use them to encourage the spirituality of the writing process.

Reflecting on the Chapter

1. What do you read and how does it correlate with what you write or want to write?

2. Which spoke of the Writer's Wheel do you most identify with in your writing?

3. Can you acknowledge your spoke as your writing strength? Why? Why not?

4. Which spoke would you like to add next to your repertoire? Why? How?

5. What do you want for yourself as a writer now, in general or in relation to the Writer's Wheel?

Writing Exercises

1. Write a short short story (less than 500 words) on a topic that interests you. When you write it, focus entirely on one spoke of the wheel. Then write it again, focusing on another spoke. Then try the other two, just to see how it feels to focus on different spokes. Which spokes come easily for you and which are difficult?

2. Write a story about the first time you fell in love, starting the natural way you would write it. Then add one element to the story

from each of the other spokes and see how that feels to you. Take out the things that seem phony. List the elements that you are drawn to from the other spokes.

Visual Exercise

Draw your own Writer's Wheel, with your favorite spoke highlighted. Next to it, write what you like about that spoke. Make an arrow in the direction of the spoke you would like to explore next.

Guided Imagery

Imagine a wise person, or the Holy, taking you on a guided tour of the Writer's Wheel within you. You visit the most familiar spoke first. Which one is it? What does it mean to you to specialize in this spoke? Your guide affirms your choice as your strength. Then your guide takes you to the other three spokes and introduces you to them. What do you learn from the tour, and from the other spokes? Your guide tells you that this is your own personal wheel and that it is there for you to use in support of your writing. Come back to the present place and write about this in your journal.

SIX

The Writer's Wheel: Forms

Finding the most applauded writing form is not a prerequisite for great writing. The Writer's Wheel honors all the forms of writing. If you honestly accept your talent as a writer, you are letting the spirituality of the writing process work, and your chances of being a great writer rise dramatically.

The Six Forms of Writing

The last chapter described the four spokes of the Writer's Wheel: spirit, technique, structure, and content. When we combine any two of these spokes, we create one of the six writing forms: entertaining, instructional, inspirational, fanciful, persuasive, and personal. Figure 9 depicts the Writer's Wheel with its four spokes and all six of the writing forms that result from combining spokes.

Entertaining Writing

Entertaining Writing results from combining technique and structure. Entertaining writers want to create a good read. They want their writing to be well-crafted, full of fine and intricate texture. They make sure to use the appropriate form, weave a compelling plot, and create a valid internal structure for the piece. Success means satisfying the reader. In fact, the main goals of this form are to give us enjoyment, provoke our thinking, let us appreciate the craft, or simply escape.

This form includes mainstream fiction, humor, short stories, drama, suspense fiction, romance fiction, westerns, and young people's fiction.

Figure 9

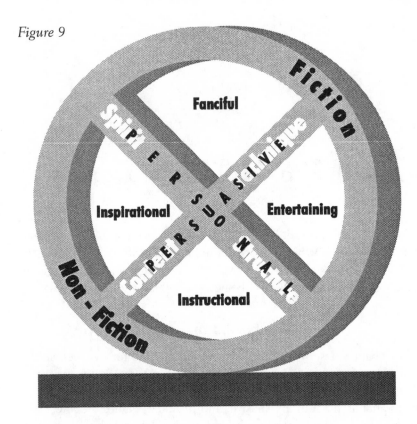

The subjects are endless and the range of styles and voices broad. Most literature classes focus on this form.

The dangers of this form are that it can be meaningless, shallow, or at its worst, pornographic. It can be technically precise but without content, or sadistically violent.

Instructional Writing

Instructional Writing emerges when we combine structure and content. Instructional writers are concerned with educating people or changing people's behavior. They are goal oriented writers, and clear about their goals. They want to help people be better at something, have more knowledge, live a better life, or think differently.

This form includes technical writing, academic writing, educational writing, documentaries, textbooks, religious writing, journalism, and how-to's, including cookbooks, health, child raising, etc. The approach is straightforward, and examples are used to illustrate rather than to tell a story.

The dangers of this form are that it can be dry, hollow, or unethical.

Inspirational Writing

Inspirational Writing results from combining the content and spirit spokes. It emphasizes possibility and taps into our hopes and feelings about life and the future. It shows us how people were in the past and how they could be in the future. Its methods are self-reflection, guidance, examination of other people's lives, and showing the world from the writer's perspective.

Here we include memoir, biography, travelogue, autobiography, spirituality, self-help, and recovery writing. The author's spirit takes a prominent role in the subject matter, and will come through in the writing.

The dangers of this form are sloppiness, preachiness, and inflated ego. Autobiographies are especially prone to ego inflation, especially if the writer's life is unexamined.

Fanciful Writing

Fanciful Writing involves the mixing of spirit and technique. It takes us out of ordinary time and space and lets us fly with the writer. Its goal is to show us things we couldn't see except at a mythical level, and take us to places only the imagination can find. It guides us into our psyche or out into the nether world. It includes fantasy, fable, fairy tale, other-world stories, science fiction, myth, folk tale, experimental oddities, and stream-of-consciousness. We not only connect with the spirit of the writer, but we go beyond the real world.

The danger of this form is getting out of touch or crazy. You may have read stream-of-consciousness writing in which the writer's stream was psychotic.

Personal Writing

Personal Writing emerges from the combination of spirit and structure. It explores the writer's interior life and brings it to the surface so others can explore theirs as well. It taps into the emotional interior, or soul, of the writer, and thus of the reader. The physical package in which the writing appears is important to personal writers. For instance, their writing is frequently contained in something else, a leather book, colorful envelope, or a musical script.

This form includes letters, poetry, songs, journals, and meditations. It brings us inside the writer, and we get to know him intimately.

The dangers of this form are that it can be self-serving, too personal, or inaccessible. The quality of writing will vary with the depth of the soul.

Persuasive Writing

Persuasive Writing results from the combination of content and technique. Persuasive writers want to convince the reader of something they believe to be important. They may want the reader to think about or do something differently as a result. They use style and technique to accomplish their goals and their writing often takes on a larger-than-life quality.

This form includes editorials, essays, political writing, commentaries, criticism, and advertising. What makes this form different from the others is that its intent is not just to inform us but to use the writing craft to persuade us.

Its dangers are dishonesty and trendiness. An example of this is criticism that serves the reviewer's own ends rather than fairly representing the piece under review.

Using the Writer's Wheel

What does elaborating the forms of writing have to do with writing well? It has to do with the spiritual concept of a calling. Most writers choose their form by asking what is acceptable to other writers or teachers, or by following the suggestions of their internal critic, rather than by asking the Holy what they are called to write. Asking the Holy is risky and challenging, but it brings us to new crossroads in our writing.

Going where we are called connects us to our writing and requires that we be fully aware of our own inner process and possibilities. One way to be aware is to ask yourself these questions:

1. Which forms am I currently reading and writing?
2. Which forms represent my writing strengths, my calling?
3. If I want to stretch myself, what are my possibilities?

In the case of my students, if they know what their writing strengths are but degrade that form of writing, they block off a creative outlet in themselves. They may have trouble developing some aspects of the Writer's Wheel because they are judging what is best. By asking the Holy what their strength is, they are moving into the spiritual process and asking for more challenges.

One student published a specialized newspaper, which was well thought of and served a niche in the community. He knew he needed a change, but he didn't know to what. He just knew he needed to write, not work as a publisher. He needed to hear his own voice instead of other people's.

But where was his voice? In class, he started writing, only to be stymied whenever he wrote anything personal. He had no problems with technical writing, but his feelings were dead. One of the assignments invited him to write to his fears. When he did, he found the log jam: severely critical voices from his family about his writing. It drew him into writing memoir to face the ghosts that haunted his mind.

The wheel can be used in several different ways, depending on your writing strengths and spiritual calling. Use the suggestions that resonate in you. They include adding a spoke, using all four spokes, moving to a new form, or moving to an opposite form.

Adding a spoke

The life of a writer has many turning points. We can be writing well and feeling satisfied when all of a sudden we discover that everything we're writing is the same. This doesn't mean we're not writing well. It is a sign of change on the horizon. The wheel can be useful during these times.

One way to stretch, change, or renew as a writer is to add a third spoke and create fuller meaning in our writing. Suppose a novelist (using technique and structure) has written several novels about rural life and feels a nagging call to add more compelling topics to her stories. She includes the effects of alcoholism in a rural, religious family in her next novel. The writer has borrowed from the content spoke and enlarged her story.

A mystery writer who borrows from other spokes is P. D. James. She writes mysteries that include compelling content and deep characterization that go beyond who committed the murder. In fact it is easy to forget who done it, but impossible to forget the details of the story and the characters' rich lives and environment.

On the other side of the wheel, let's say a writer works mainly on biography (content and spirit). If he were to give us some scenes from the person's life as he imagines they happened, based on the facts he has accumulated (thus adding technique), the biography would have an added dimension. Irving Stone's *The Agony and the Ecstasy* does this. Michelangelo's life and art come alive when the reader gets inside of his struggles with his family and with the pope.

Using all four spokes

Using all four spokes of the wheel results in great or miraculous writing, and it is wonderful to behold. When using all four spokes becomes natural, it feels like a combination of power and ecstasy. L'Engle would say that it means the writer is listening. I think this comes with maturation, deeply felt experience, and powerful craft.

Two examples of this are Alice Walker's *The Color Purple* and Norman Maclean's *A River Runs Through It*. Walker's book is a novel (technique, structure) including significant material about racism and abuse (content), and she sends us this story from her heart (spirit). Maclean's book is a memoir (content, spirit) that also attends to technique and structure by beautifully mingling religious imagery with fly fishing, and then weaving his brother's death into the entire tapestry to give the story structure.

Moving to an adjacent form

Another way to use the wheel is to switch to a form adjacent to the one we know. A science fiction writer may write inspirational books for teenagers, a cookbook writer may try short stories or humorous stories about food, or a novelist may write educational books about writing. These can be difficult moves because the writers are learning new forms instead of adding something extra to their own forms. The learning process will be different, because each form has its own internal rules.

Carolyn Heilbrun and William Zinsser are writers who cross over to adjacent forms, writing both fiction and instructional books. Heilbrun wrote a classic book on androgyny, *Toward a Theory of Androgyny,* and also writes mysteries under the name Amanda Cross. William Zinsser is a journalist who writes fiction, non-fiction, and humor, including a book on writing, *On Writing Well,* and a novel, *The Paradise Bit.*

Moving to an opposite form

If we want to move to a totally different form than the one we know best, we can jump to the opposite side of the wheel. A poet may switch to political essays, a writer of technical manuals may cross over to fables, or a romance writer may switch to spiritual essays. These are larger jumps, but fun and worth the learning they require.

Examples of authors who've crossed to opposite forms are Lillian Hellman, who wrote plays and memoirs, Leo Tolstoy, who wrote novels and memoirs, Madeleine L'Engle, who writes fantasy and instructional books, C.S. Lewis, who wrote fables, memoirs, and instructional books, and Isaac Asimov, who wrote in all forms. If you want the ultimate writing challenge, change forms *and* use all four spokes. You will feel transformed.

In my own case, after publishing several nonfiction books in the instructional and inspirational forms, I felt I was in a rut, and my soul was languishing. I took classes in three other forms to see which attracted me. Some did, some didn't. I started writing humor, fables, and fiction, along with nonfiction. I felt excited again. In this book, which is primarily instructional (although some might say it's persuasive), I use mostly the content and structure spokes, but I borrowed the central metaphor of the Writer's Wheel, along with many illustrations and examples, from the technique spoke to make the concepts more accessible and personal.

Of course, writers can be perfectly satisfied with staying in a single form and borrowing from other spokes, so that they write about different people and interesting subjects, using new styles or different structures and voices. The point is, *it's up to the writer* and what she or he is called to write.

The Writer's Wheel suggests the twin ideas of movement and balance, either within the same form or among forms. In order to move or change, we need to be open. In order to stay in balance, we need to appreciate where we are. I suggest to my students and to myself that if we would take the energy that we spend worrying about which forms are best and which ones we "should" be writing in, and put that energy instead into listening to the Holy and becoming great writers, no one would focus on forms anymore.

Reflecting on the Chapter

1. Do you believe there is one correct form that produces great writing? Which one? Do you write in that form?

2. What form do you use most for your writing? How do you feel about that form?

3. Which form scares you when you think about using it? Why?

4. If you were to stretch as a writer, what form would you move to, or which spokes would you add? Why?

Writing Exercises

1. Pick a topic you enjoy. Write the following using that topic:
   - A headline for a newspaper
   - A two-stanza poem
   - A title and chapter titles for a novel
   - The plot to a murder mystery
   - An essay title and outline

- A letter to a friend
- A biography title and subject

Which one or two of these came easily and which were a challenge? What does that tell you about the form you are most drawn to?

2. Describe a person you hate, a person you love, and a person you've observed from afar. Use any form you are naturally drawn to and observe how you feel about the writing. Then choose an opposite form and try to write on the same topics. See if it feels different to write in that form. That is an example of stretching.

Visual exercise

Draw the Writer's Wheel with forms, highlighting the one that is yours. Place a star in the one you read most. That is a clue to what you are drawn to. Do the two coincide?

Guided Imagery

Go in your imagination to a place you like to rest. Listen for the Holy to come and be beside you. Notice that the Holy brought you a piece of writing and gives it to you. It is a package of all the different writing forms on a single topic, you.

You page through the package. It contains poems, a novel, biography, a documentary, letters, essays, fables, all about you. You realize that you appear in a myriad of forms and it touches you deeply. You page through again and choose the form that appeals to your heart, that beckons you to write. You make note of which form that is. Come back to the present and write about the experience in your journal.

Soul and Critique

Feedback is potentially the most supportive and the most lethal experience of any writer. Damaging critique has caused more people to quit writing than any other factor I know of. Most of us can remember damaging criticism from well-meaning people all the way back to early childhood. I have been a participant in writing classes in which half the class dropped out by the third week because of the type and style of feedback perpetrated or allowed by the teacher. Does this mean writers are just not tough enough, not thick skinned enough? Some teachers would endorse that philosophy. Many journalists thrive on it. I don't.

A friend and I, both published writers, took a class together to explore writing forms other than our own. In this class, my friend wrote a poem for the first time in over twenty years, a delicate poem about shells and the sea shore. When she read it in class, a student said, "I'd suggest you write a poem that doesn't rhyme." I could see my friend's face flush and I sensed her humiliation. No one else said anything, not even the teacher.

I'm not suggesting that rhymed poems are popular these days, or that they're always well done, but this poem came from inside of her. The student's narrow view, that rhyming makes bad poetry, was inappropriate to my friend's writing process.

If the teacher wanted her to keep writing and someday experiment with unrhymed poems, the best way to get her started would have been to support her in her current work and challenge her toward the next step, whatever that might have been. He could have countered the student's comments by mentioning T.S. Eliot's cat poems, the whole world of famous limericks, not to mention Shakespeare's sonnets.

I believe that harsh, negative, and unjustified feedback—feedback that is more for the aggrandizement of the giver than the receiver—severely damages the soul of the writer, and that even if that writer does go on to write, he will have lost a part of himself that will take a long time to retrieve.

Yet I also believe that feedback is crucial to the writing process and will help the writing move closer to what the writer intended. How do we reconcile the need for feedback with the lethal way in which so much feedback is given?

Dorothy DeLay teaches violin virtuosos at Julliard. She has worked with students as strikingly different as Itzhak Perlman and Nigel Kennedy, a punk-style classical violinist. Her philosophy is to never criticize, but rather to pull out of her students what is unique to them and to encourage and challenge them to hone it for themselves.

What are the results of that? Students who are excited about their uniqueness, unafraid of doing something different from what the teacher does, willing to experiment, confident and creative. Their souls are lifted up and set free, not constrained to be a person someone else can live through vicariously. The idea is to uplift, support, challenge, encourage, pull, and deepen, not do the opposite, which is to mold, project, toughen, straighten out, shape, or discourage.

What Makes Negative Critique Lethal to the Soul?

If feedback is important, why is it potentially so harmful to us? Because when we write, we put our souls on paper. So when people give us feedback, it is our soul they are addressing. We need to keep this in mind, lest we rip the soul to shreds inadvertently or unknowingly.

Three kinds of feedback are particularly lethal.

The first comes from writers who have not worked enough with their inner critics to know how their critics function and how damaging they can be. During feedback opportunities, whether formal or informal, the inner critics of both the giver and the receiver can grab hold and work their destruction. The critiquer may not even be conscious of these antics. I have heard devastating and unjustifiable things said to writers, things that clearly have more to do with the speaker's inner critic than with the work being critiqued. I am always alert to people in my classes who have harsh critics, because I know they are damaging to that person but also seek insatiably to hurt others.

The second form of lethal feedback is projection, which has little to do with the writing but instead emerges from the jealousy and insecurity of the reader. Many writers wish they could write like someone else in class, and therefore feel insecure about their own writing. Their feedback is either too solicitous (and mostly useless) or deliberately critical, to get back at the other writer for being so good. Neither of these is useful to the writer and both reinforce the insecurity of the giver.

The third and potentially most lethal form of feedback is from a teacher or from any authority figure. Students put more weight on the feedback of someone who is published, or who has degrees or experience. That makes the unreflective teacher's biases and opinions, both negative and positive, extremely dangerous. When teachers or authority figures are unaware of their biases, their voices, their opinions, they project to the students the idea there is only one way to write in order to write well.

This is simply not true, and moves the students toward group voice, in which everyone ends up writing like the teacher. It illustrates the insecurity of the teacher and it means the death of the students' souls.

Sometimes it works the opposite way. Teachers are so aware of their biases that their awareness limits their writing and teaching. I heard of a fiction writing teacher who will not work with suspense fiction writers. He says it is because he is unfamiliar of the form, but it creates the impression that he does not believe mystery writers can develop the craft of writing. It suggests that even though he is a teacher of craft, he is content driven, not craft driven. Think of the transformation that could occur in that teacher and in his students if he decided to help mystery writers develop the craft of fiction and let *them* create the suspense and plot.

What Helps Writers Thrive?

The atmosphere surrounding writing is crucial to its outcome. I believe the atmosphere that best promotes great writing is a spiritual one. Thinking of the writing process as sacred and of the soul as the primary vehicle of writing helps us to honor the writer and the writing. In order to make the atmosphere supportive as well as challenging, it is useful to consider the writing setting holy and the writer gifted.

My major challenge in writing classes is to help writers listen to their writing, heed their souls, and trust both themselves and the spiritual process of writing. This requires that reverence be the order of the day, because it calls forth mutual respect as well as laughter, tears, and even anger at ourselves. I encourage that atmosphere by such things as thanking writers after they read something in front of the class; giving writers time to talk about their writing, even if they didn't bring something to read; giving personal homework assignments as well as general ones; reading out loud about the ups and downs of other writers; and sharing my own vulnerability about writing and publishing. The first hour of class is for discussion and the sharing of ideas, experiences, and principles. The second hour is for reading what writers brought to class.

Sometimes I start class with a time of silence, then read an invocation such as this: "This is soul time. The space is sacred and the ground, even when it quakes, is holy. We ask the Holy to be attentive to us on our spiritual journey as we embrace our critics and wrestle with our angels. These words we speak in awe, reverence, and expectation, knowing that all will be well. Amen."

I attend to process closely, asking people to be aware of their inner critic when someone else is reading, and asking them to talk about that. And I ask each person to take a risk as part of the class, a risk that is appropriate for them. It helps the rest of us to know what the risk is and to talk about how it went.

By far the most important and vulnerable time in class is when a writer has finished reading and there is dead silence. This is the time the soul comes timidly or boldly out of the person and waits for our reaction. It is an honor to us that the soul took the risk to emerge and it is our responsibility to support and challenge it without crippling it.

I believe writers already know, either consciously or subconsciously, eighty-five percent of the information that will take their writing to the next place. I use that as my guide when I respond to the writing. In beginning classes, I ask class members not to give feedback on the writing. Instead, I ask writers what they are going to read and then ask them one of several questions afterward, depending on what and how they read. I do that so writers will know it is safe to take risks and so they will learn to listen to themselves, and trust themselves, instead of depending on what others think.

These questions are designed to help writers probe themselves and their writing to find the answers they already know. Other class members can relax, since they don't have to think of something to say, or they must discipline themselves not to blurt out ideas, but rather learn from the other writers' issues.

Here are samples of the questions I ask less experienced writers after they've read their work:

- How did it feel to read the piece out loud?
- What other ideas or thoughts did the writing tap in you?
- Stay with the strong reaction you had. Talk about it or write directly to the feeling in your journal.
- What part of the piece did you like most? Why?
- How did your inner critic respond to the writing?
- How did your angel respond?
- Describe your voice. Does it feel like your own?
- Where does this piece want to go next? What is tugging at you?
- What are you holding back?

With more experienced writers, I might add one of these questions:

- What further questions does this piece raise in you?
- Where does it resonate in you and why?
- Do you feel a sense of relief, release, or peace after this writing? If so, keep moving with it.
- Do you feel frustration, anger, depression, or fear? If so, ask what the piece is probing in you that you are resisting? Be gentle.
- What part is calling for change, doesn't feel done, wants to expand?
- If this piece is finished, can you let it be finished?
- Is this piece calling for a change in form? Does it want to take you to a new place on the Writer's Wheel?

- What is your intent with this piece?
- How does it fit with other pieces you're writing? Is it part of a larger series?
- What specifically do you want from me, from us, for feedback?
- Does this piece want to be public? In what way?

For both groups, and for myself, it helps to remember that this is the writer's piece, not ours. I say, every once in awhile, "Remember, it is your piece."

For Writers Who Are Ready to Ask for Feedback

I encourage writers to ask for feedback from others, but only when they are ready and only when they realize in their hearts that they already know eighty-five percent of what they need to know to write well. It helps to be confident that the piece we're writing is our, not our teacher's or our spouse's or our writing friends'. That means we're at a point in the drafts, or in our confidence level, where feedback won't drastically alter the piece unless we agree with it wholeheartedly.

One time to ask for feedback is when you know you need an expert opinion on some aspect of your work which is new or foreign to you. You may need facts to complete your story: the details of a local celebration, the characteristics of certain trees that grow in Asia, the date of a world event. Or you may need to know how to make a scene more suspenseful. Advice like this can come from books or from individuals and usually is objective.

Another time to seek feedback is when you're stuck on a piece and are unsure why. The first place to seek help from is your angel (see chapters 9 and 12). Ask your angel what you're afraid of or who is stalling you. Ask yourself what would happen if you moved ahead. If these ideas don't work, go to a nurturing writing friend or teacher and see if you can sort out what the call is for you in the stuckness. Being stuck is usually a sign of an impending breakthrough if you stay with it and don't abandon the writing.

A great time to get feedback is at the crossroads of near-completion. This is the time when you have said most of what you want to say in the way you want to say it but may be unsure what else you want to say. You feel good about the general writing but have some questions you can't answer because you're too close to the piece. This is a time to put together a list of specific questions and get feedback.

Typical questions are: What is the tone of this piece? What is the main point? How do you experience Jim (one of the main characters)? Is he distinct or blurry? Does the idea come across clearly? Is it persuasive? Is the illustration clear? When did you figure out the secret? Was that too soon for you? What do you feel from this poem? What is it about?

Choosing the right people to ask for feedback is very important. They need to be people you respect and trust, people you believe will help you, not maim you. Vicious people give vicious feedback. Respectful people give respectful feedback. I sort people into three groups when I'm looking for feedback on my work: content experts, the typical audience for my piece, and writers I trust. We need different people for different things.

It doesn't help to give a science fiction story to someone who doesn't like science fiction. It's hard to give helpful feedback if you don't like the content. When I read a section of my golf mystery to my poetry group, one member said, "Why would anyone want to write a book about golf?" Obviously, she would not be one of my readers.

It helps to ask different questions of the different groups: content questions of the experts, writing questions of the writers, and form and style questions of the audience for the piece. I recommend never asking simply, "What do you think?" It leaves you vulnerable to the biases and whims of the reader and doesn't pinpoint what you are questioning yourself. I did that a few times and felt the darts of venom piercing my heart. One woman, after reading my whole novel, asked, "How do you know enough to write about sexy women?" There was only one scene in which a sensual woman appeared.

Using Feedback Constructively

Once you've solicited feedback, the next important question is how to use it. Sixty percent of the feedback you'll receive is very straightforward, and you'll say to yourself, "Of course. Why didn't I see that?" That is the most useful kind of feedback. Make those changes and see how they resonate in you. They probably will come as a relief, or will answer a question that was troubling you.

You will also get feedback you are not sure of, feedback that does-n't give you an obvious *aha!* My rule of thumb is that when two people cite the same issue, confusion, or question, it is worth looking at. What if only one person cites something? That is more complicated and your own internal critic may come in handy in these cases. Ask your critic to help you see the truth in the feedback you've received and separate it from the biases of these particular readers.

Let's say you are writing inspirational pieces and using several stories to illustrate your points. An academic reader suggests that you ought to quote more sources, more well-known people. You don't understand what that would do to strengthen the piece. Your critic reminds you that academic writers always quote multiple sources. That is what makes writing credible to them. So this might be a bias of the reader that is not useful to your piece. Your critic also reminds you that you have used several examples already. It is not disrespectful to your readers not to use all of their feedback.

It helps to be aware of unwarranted projection by other writers or readers. This usually comes from unresolved issues they are having and has nothing to do with you, although it is hard to see that sometimes. When feedback isn't related to the piece, or when the tone of the feedback is jarring, it's usually projection.

A jarring tone may be angry, anxious, or elitist. One man read my manuscript on leading from the soul and said, "You can't say that in corporations." I laughed inside because, of course, he was saying that *he* couldn't say what I had said. He was inside a corporation. I was not and could say whatever I believed without putting my job on the line.

What to Do When Asked for Feedback

When someone asks you for feedback, think of it as the writer's soul asking you to help it move to the next place. Be respectful and prayerful. See the experience as sacred ground. If you cannot do this, you would be better off not giving feedback. If the writer really wants the help, support, and challenge, you have an opportunity to propel her soul forward or to thwart it for a season. That is an awesome responsibility.

My guidelines for giving feedback that people specifically ask for is to do it as respectfully and honestly as possible, trying not to project the unresolved issues of my critic. One way to do this is to use only descriptive words and stay far away from evaluative ones. Evaluative words include: phony, trite, beautiful, sentimental, wordy, garbage, ordinary, corny, non-literary, shallow, formulaic, wonderful, genre, minimalist, traditional, sloppy. You get the point.

Descriptive words are much more useful, not as loaded, and give the writer something to work with. Descriptive words include clear, hazy, angry, detailed, spare, concrete, dense, sensual, calm, confusing, humorous, detached, persuasive, fast-paced, personal, evocative.

What the writer needs to know is how the piece affected you personally, where you were moved or persuaded, where you lost contact. This encourages you to use "I" statements and to be as specific as possible, basing your criticism on the intent of the writer and the nature of the piece. To give useful feedback you may have to go beyond your personal opinion, especially if you are not representative of the audience for the piece. If the piece is all dry humor and you don't like dry humor, but it is still well written, you can say you think the writer is very adept at dry humor, even though that isn't your brand. An unreflective reviewer would say the piece lacked effective humor without seeing his own bias.

If it's difficult for you to give feedback, stick to "I" statements pertaining to the piece instead of the writer. Here are several examples:

- First, let me say I applaud you for writing this. I was struck by the clarity of your writing, and the plausibility. Here are a few questions I had . . .
- I'm confused by ...
- I'm captivated by this idea. How about an example to illustrate it ...
- I want to know more about this character, her ..., her ..., her ...
- The piece changes direction dramatically for me at paragraph three and I had to go back a few times to get oriented to the new ideas. Is that intentional?
- You're courageous to write about this idea. I'm proud of you for taking it on so directly.
- This dialogue confuses me. I lost track of who is saying what.
- I lost my concentration in chapter three. I think I needed dialogue or movement to break up the description.
- I am drawn to your sensuous descriptions. All my senses were involved.

- In the poem, the word leaky stands out to me like it wants something. I'm not sure why.

Feedback is not only useful, but necessary. Think of feedback as thoughtful pruning in a deeply loved garden. It helps us make our creations even better. Our souls are intimately involved in the feedback process and therefore we do well to be conscious of both the way we give feedback and the way we ask for it. Our well-being and our writing depend on it.

Reflecting on the Chapter

1. When have you experienced critique that has crippled your soul?

2. How can you nurture yourself when you ask for feedback?

3. How can you structure feedback so it is useful to your writing?

4. What are the key questions you need to ask of your particular writing project now?

5. How can you use your spirituality to manage feedback effectively?

6. When will you be able to call yourself a writer?

7. Who are the people you trust to read your writing and give you feedback?

Writing Exercises

1. My worst writing experience was ...

2. The best idea I've ever had was ...

3. The criticism I had of my writing ten years ago was ...

4. The criticism I have of my writing today is …

5. I feel joy from my writing when …

6. Write fifteen non-evaluative words you can use to describe writing.

Visual Exercise

Balcony people are people who applaud you and encourage you to keep going. Draw a balcony, then put your balcony people in it. (They can all be stick people) Write their names so you can remember them.

Guided Imagery

Go to a quiet, safe, and comfortable place. In your imagination, see yourself at a reading. You are reading out loud, to other people, a piece that you love. Another writer stands up and criticizes you because the piece isn't political enough. You see an imaginary critic on his shoulder, screaming in his ear, telling him what to say to you. You sympathize with the man for having such a harsh critic. Another person stands and wishes you'd say more about the main character's inner search. You see an angel on her shoulder, whispering in her ear. You feel a warmth around your neck and ache to go deeper with your main character, to let your character take you there. You decide to listen to the second reviewer. You are relieved and satisfied. You come back from your imagination. You feel good for having discerned the critic from the angel. Now write about it.

EIGHT

Embracing Your Critic

An editor invited a student of mine to submit an article to a magazine that she'd written for previously. She wrote it promptly and turned it in one week before the deadline, only to have it rejected and returned immediately. Three weeks after the deadline, the editor called and said, "Where's that article? You said it would be here weeks ago." My student explained the situation and submitted the article again, only to have it rejected again. Then the magazine was sold and she gave up.

Some people have experiences like this and never write again; others shrug their shoulders and go on. But we all remember our negative writing experiences, and for many of us, the pain of them lingers for years.

The lingering pain is the work of our ever-active critic. The critic damages us more than the actual event does, sometimes by mumbling harsh words in our ears as we sit down to write, sometimes by popping up in the middle of a good story. The critic will continue to haunt us until we learn to actively embrace it.

All of us who write have critics on our shoulders, and the single goal of those critics is to destroy our confidence. Writing is a process in which we put our souls on paper, so when the critic attacks our souls, it delivers a nearly fatal blow. How does the critic work? It whispers lies in our ear whenever we think about writing. It gets louder when we consider reading our writing to others. It destroys in two ways, by telling us why we can't write in the first place, and then if we go ahead and put pen to paper, by telling us that what we said is stupid or worthless.

Common sense would tell you to get rid of your critic by ignoring it or destroying it. Unfortunately, it isn't that simple. The critic will not go away just because you will it to. I suggest learning to honor the truth that your critic, in its fumbling way, is asking you to hear.

Why would anyone want to embrace the critic, a symbol that holds so much negative possibility? Because if you don't know the critic intimately, it can hurt you much more easily. And because if you befriend the critic, you can use it to make your writing more effective, instead of spending your energy in a constant battle with it. By embracing anything we fear and by knowing it intimately, we take the sting out of it and obtain its power.

I am suggesting that you take a daring, spiritual approach, asking the Holy to help you face and engage your critic. Embracing the critic means speaking to it, holding it close, learning what it wants, what its best weapons are, where it hangs out, why it thinks the way it does, where it came from and how it makes you vulnerable. Then you can more freely understand how to get it to back off when you don't want it around (which is usually for the first few drafts); how to encourage it to take a long-needed vacation when you want to be especially prolific; and how to engage it when you really need it in the writing process. But remember, when you make a pledge to your critic that you will use it later, keep the pledge. Critics want to be appreciated too.

Remembering the Critic's Antics

Early in my writing classes, I ask my students to describe their negative writing experiences. Most people can remember junior high or high school experiences. Everyone remembers current ones. These are the stuff of the critic, and in order to heal, we need to conjure them up, even if they are painful. A bad experience may be inflicted initially by an external source, but in a flash it settles into our psyches, asserting that we are worthless.

Andrea's high school English teacher read her story out loud in front of the class, exaggerating her use of the phrase "many stone" for minestrone soup, a central pun in her tale. At the end he arched his head back and shouted, "This is the stupidest thing I have ever heard," and threw the paper across the room.

Jack wrote a striking short story about child sexual abuse, centered around a dream a teenager had about her abusive father. The class was riveted by his reading of the story and he eagerly awaited his instructor's critique. The teacher said, "I think you should take the dream out of the story."

When Carrie was a college student, she was wildly enthusiastic about creative writing. Her teachers were supportive, and she even submitted stories for the school's literary review. When she showed one of her best stories to her father, he read it and said, "Why don't you spend your time writing something real—and practical. This is just a waste of time." Carrie slowly shut down until by college graduation she wasn't writing at all.

Dave worked for two years on a novel about his passion, rugby. Feeling stuck, he took a chapter to his writers' support group to get their feedback so he could gain courage to complete the book. When he finished reading the most exciting chapter, one member looked at him and said, "Why write about a sport people aren't interested in?"

In junior high, I had great enthusiasm for special projects involving decorative covers made of colored paper, with pictures and large lettering. One of these projects was for a home economics class and was about desserts. I worked hard on the project, selected just the right picture for the cover and then wrote in large black letters across the top, DESERTS. When I got the book back, my teacher had inserted a large red S next to the other S, ruining my cover and snuffing out my enthusiasm for any such projects in the future.

These painful events build up an inner belief that we are not good writers and that what we have to say is worthless. Family members, friends, or other writers frequently add to the problem with well-intentioned advice or feedback. It results in a solid, crusty critic inside us, firmly internalized and ready to pounce whenever we gather the courage to write.

Every writer's critic has its own ways of appearing. Some speak in quiet nagging voices whenever we think about writing or actually sit down to write. Others remind us that we are not real writers; *other* people are real writers. If that doesn't work, it tells us our lives aren't worth writing about. The compulsive critic edits every word we use, suggesting that there is a better one but that we'll never find it. Another suggests that if we were really good writers we'd be writing in a different form. If we're presently writing fiction, we should be writing poetry. If we write poetry, we should be writing essays. The critic has clever and devious ways of tormenting us, distracting us, demeaning us, and judging us harshly. In my experience, writers with the harshest critics are English majors, editors who are frustrated writers, first-born children, and people from undiagnosed dysfunctional families.

Naming and Embracing Your Critic

Your critic usually is both inside of you and outside of you. The inner critic is the accumulation of all those negative messages about yourself and your writing, frequently personified by one or two people in your past. It emerges as a voice in your head that critiques you mercilessly. It affects your self-esteem and gets internalized as a ferocious negative force. The outer critic is usually an overly critical or abusive person in your life who criticizes or ridicules your work, inadvertently or deliberately. I call them poisonous people. Unexamined inner and outer critics are lethal to your writing.

Sometimes your current outer critic is someone very close to you—a spouse, friend, parent, or teacher. I warn students not to give their work to poisonous people because they can kill the work. This does not mean that you should never seek feedback, but you should never seek it from lethal sources, whether they are well meaning or not.

One good way to learn more about your critic is to name it, whether it is a person or an abstraction to you. I call my critic Rude. One friend calls hers Jake, another, Gloom. By giving it a name, you make it more manageable and identifiable, someone with whom you can begin a relationship.

Once you have named your critic, invite it to write or speak to you in your journal. Ask all the questions you can think of to get it to expose itself to you: Who are you? What do you want from me? Why do you act the way you do? Where did you come from? What do you like? What do you dislike? Where am I most vulnerable to you? How can I befriend you?

Listen to your critic and write its responses in your journal, painful as that might be. You will learn a great deal of valuable information, which you can use later. Write back and ask more questions, probing the critic's feelings and reasoning. When you can stop fighting with the critic and engage it personally, the process of transformation begins. It will be worth the effort. It will bring you courage and deepen your writing.

One woman wrote to her critic and found out it was her twin sister, who tried to outdo her in every aspect of her life. When she began to write poetry, her twin sister took it up too and told her she'd better find something else to do. She took that advice and for ten years didn't write a single poem.

Don called forth his critic only to find out it was his alcoholic mother, for whom nothing was ever enough. After he had published four nonfiction books, she said to him, laughing, "When are you going to write something I can enjoy?"

Some critics are more subtle, as Jane found out. She always felt she was a good writer until she began writing stories that took on some tough subjects. The other writers in her writers' group were hesitant to comment on her writing. She took it as a sign of disapproval and began questioning her writing. After consulting with a former writing teacher and writing in her journal, she talked to a few of members of her group privately and discovered that they were simply afraid of taking on difficult topics.

Minimizing the Critic's Power

To make sacred the process of getting to know your critic, bring your faith and courage into the process. Not only will this minimize the critic's effects, it will call forth deeper parts of you. Honor that process by making it part of your writing life.

One practice my students use successfully is the creation of writing rituals, including supportive objects, symbols, and reminders of what it means for them to write. Photos, posters, quotes, candles, angels, or music work well. Other people like special chairs or a private space with a view. Some need a special tea or a pet in the room. Experiment to see what works for you and ask others what they've tried.

Another useful practice is to quiet down, meditate, or pray before you begin writing. Bless your writing and the space. This reduces the chatter in your head and calms the critic as well. It clears your mind to concentrate on the piece, the reason you are writing it, and the spiritual call it has for you. Remember, you are cultivating your gift of writing.

You might also try this: On the left side of a sheet of paper, list all the things the critic tells you about yourself and your writing. Then on the right side, counter each statement with a reasonable positive statement related to it. If the critic says, "You have nothing to say," you can reply, "Everyone, including me, has something to say and it is important that I say it." When you have countered each statement, rip the paper in half from top to bottom. Toss the left side away and tape the right side in your journal or on your computer. Read the statements whenever your critic gets active.

Both I and others have found it helpful to speak directly and honestly to the critic about what it is doing to you, just as you would to another human being. When I was writing about domestic violence, my critic got very active. I told it, "I hear you sniping at me and telling me it's futile and stupid to write about this. You told me the same thing last week. What I really think is that you're afraid of what I might say—afraid that I will tell too much or get too personal. Well, I feel very strongly about this topic and it's part of my healing process to write about it publicly. What I'm saying is true and important. So please calm down and help me later with the editing. Okay?" My critic backed down and the piece was stirring, both for me and, apparently, for many readers, who told me they appreciated my candor and vulnerability.

Sometimes I take the opposite approach, holding my critic lovingly in my lap, asking it gently what it is afraid of. If it feels safe, it is more willing to speak. There is a soft underbelly to every critic, if you can only find it. I know people who write to their critics, sing to them, woo them, or give them other activities to keep them occupied. Whatever you choose to do, it is helpful to get to the feeling level with the critic so you can get to the heart of the matter. What is it afraid of, angry at, hurt by, revengeful towards? Going to the core feeling helps release the pent-up energy in the critic's innards. Candor, courage, and honesty are the keys to the release.

The escape route can also help you minimize your critic. You can get up and think while you are refilling your coffee cup, luring the critic to the kitchen and asking it to stay there while you finish writing. Or you can go for a walk and get the critic out of your system. One woman calls her friend's answering machine just to listen to her voice, because it gives her the courage to keep writing.

Using Your Critic as Writing Assistant

Once the critic knows you will not neglect it or kill it, it will find a nice, quiet spot in the room and either just sit there or do something to occupy its mind until you need it. It's like having another person in the room, or a cat who wants to be where you are and needs only minimal contact.

Sooner or later, you must honor your critic by using it for tasks that will help your writing. The critic loves to be needed, and the grooming, editing, and polishing aspects of writing lend themselves to the critic's skills. Once you get your ideas down, get the story line done, or finish the first few drafts of a poem, you can invite the critic into the process.

Critics are also great at sorting out how to use feedback. Some editors mark a manuscript aggressively and make what seem to be unwarranted changes. Your critic can help you decide which changes are necessary. It can also help you see the issue from the editor's point of view and find a better way to make your point.

Critics need direct and specific guidelines. Ask the critic to remind you to use the spell check rather than telling you that you are a bad speller. Ask the critic to help you find a good editor rather than railing at you for not knowing all the rules of grammar. Ask the critic to find the right metaphor instead of complaining about your use of imagery.

Use the energy of the critic by asking it: What further questions does this piece raise? Where does the work want to expand or contract? Where is my voice fearful or timid? Did I say what I really wanted to say? Could I write this from a different point of view or in a different form and get to its soul more effectively?

When you establish boundaries for your critic and hold it to the agreement you've made, the critic will surprise you by becoming an ally. When you transform the negative power of the critic into useful energy, it releases you to greater writing.

How do you know if your struggle with the critic is paying off? You will be able to write in your own voice, even if few people around you have a similar voice or appreciate yours. Or you will find that you can hear other people read their work and applaud them without automatically thinking that they are better or worse than you. You will no longer project your hurt or anger onto other writers through harsh or unjustified feedback. You will begin writing in a form or genre that appeals to you, even though you risk disapproval for it. You will believe that you have something important to say and that you are the person to say it, even if saying it is difficult. You will face the fear of writing, knowing that by writing anyway you will thrive.

Reflecting on the Chapter

1. Have you ever experienced writer's block? Describe it.

2 Who or what first discouraged you in your writing? What effect did that have on you?

3. What does your critic tell you? What bad thing does it say will happen to you if you write?

4. How do you counteract that voice?

5. What is in your heart to write now?

6. What will happen if you write it?

7. How can you make your critic a writing assistant?

Writing Exercises

1. Write to your critic in your journal. Ask these questions and let it answer you:

   Who are you?
   What do you want from me?
   Why do you act the way you do?
   Where did you come from?
   What do you like?
   What do you dislike?
   Where am I most vulnerable to you?
   How can I befriend you?

2. What are you most proud of in your writing? Most satisfied with?

3. How does your critic respond when you write this?

5. My worst fear about writing is ...

Visual exercise

Describe your critic by drawing it. Name it.

Guided Imagery

Sit in a safe, quiet place until you are ready to have a contact with your critic. Be aware of your breathing. Tell yourself this is sacred ground. Ask the Holy to attend to you. Invite your critic to speak to you. Ask the critic why it haunts you. Listen and write down what it says. Hear the critic, but remember that you are big enough to respond to it. You don't have to take this inside, just listen to it. Tell your critic that you hear what it says but that this is not what you need it for; you have other tasks for it, and your angel is helping you to do what you need to do to write. Thank your critic for coming to see you. Stay in that safe place for five minutes and take in the experience. Be kind and gentle with yourself. Write about this in your journal.

NINE

≈

Wrestling with Your Angel

Just as we have a critic on one shoulder, we have an angel on the other, whose only goal is to help our writing take on its greatness. It does this by wooing us to our passion. Ironically, this usually involves a struggle— a life-giving struggle, but a struggle nevertheless. It is strange that we embrace our critic and struggle with our angel, but that is what I observe and experience to be true.

Wrestling with the angel can be even more challenging than embracing the critic, because the angel tell us liberating truth, even if it is painful, and holds the key to our brilliance, which I believe frightens us to our core. The angel wants to give us a gift but cannot do so unless we claim it, which involves an internal struggle to let go of our fears and accept the gift the angel offers. In that intimate struggle, we find out who we are and we unleash our writing passion.

Poets, artists, and holy books all inform us about the role of angels, which historically has been to inform, announce, guide, comfort, and protect us. They don't mention the intimate relationship we develop with our angels, and that is what intrigues me most, intimacy with our angel, whether that angel is a metaphor or a presence in or beyond our psyches. Our angel can be our own inner voice (the accumulation of positive figures, loving people, self esteem), real people in our lives who love us, the spirits of people who have died but act as nurturers and guides, or a spirit messenger from the Holy. It can take many roles; guide, challenger, warning figure, supporter, nurturer. It is helpful to identify the angel in our lives.

But to gain intimacy, we must allow the angel to be more than guide and comfort. We must engage with it at a deeper, more vulnerable level, asking for the courage to face ourselves, try the unknown, and risk the disapproval of people close to us. We must wrestle with our angel. This struggle, if we are persistent, results in a gift, releasing our passion and greatness as writers. This is soul writing, the inevitable result of a well-attended spiritual journey.

Wrestling with our angel involves three central themes that relate directly to the intimacy and the spirituality of the writing process: discovering how our shadow blocks our writing; experiencing the gift of great and courageous writing; and giving writing a sacred place in our lives.

How Our Shadows Block Our Writing

When we begin wrestling with our angels, we discover our own dark shadows, the hidden parts of ourselves that sabotage us and hinder our writing process. We understand how our own woundedness is a step in our journey to wholeness. If we are perpetually angry or cynical, we can look at the source of that rage within us and learn to funnel the anger constructively into our writing. Looking at what we dislike in others, we can recognize those behaviors as things in us that need attention. If we can't stand wimpy behavior in others, we can look at our own frightened inner child, who desperately wants to grow up and write courageously. If we hate arrogance, we can uncover the immense insecurity our own arrogance has covered up and observe where that honesty takes us in our writing.

Embracing the pain at our core while not letting it determine our lives releases the passion and greatness that also resides there, under the blankets of hurt, fear, and shame. Writers who have touched their core are indelibly marked by the process and describe it graphically. In *Teaching a Stone to Talk*, Annie Dillard says:

> "In the deeps are the violence and terror of which psychology has warned us. But if you ride these monsters deeper down, if you drop with them farther over the world's rim, you find what our sciences cannot locate or name, the substrate, the ocean or matrix or ether which buoys the rest, which gives goodness its power for good, and evil its power for evil, the unified field: our complex and inexplicable caring for each other, and for our life together here. This is given. It is not learned."

Wherever our journey leads us, it is our willingness to take the step into the fear, into the shadows, that begins our wrestling match with our angel, who is there in the darkness, waiting to give us our gift and release our passion. This wrestling match needs support and encouragement from others: family, friends, writing teachers, therapists, spiritual directors. Most of all, we need support from the Holy, who provides us with the courage to sustain the effort. The journey and the wrestling are different for each individual and must be treated uniquely.

How do writers accept the angel's invitation to wrestle, find their shadow, heal the wounds? In a wide variety of ways. Dreams that come up in the course of our lives will, if we work with them consciously, lead us to our subconscious truths. Unexpected moments of insight or pain can do the same thing. Writing on subjects we are afraid of can offer a rich source of the angel's wisdom, as can accepting things we find despicable in others as unresolved parts of ourselves.

Anita, a middle-aged woman in my writing class, described sitting at a dance recital in which she was thoroughly enraptured. In her words:

> "A very old, white-haired woman was being escorted to the seat next to me. She sat down with great difficulty, her heavy breathing signaling the feat. Her presence was further punctuated by the saliva that fell from the corner of her mouth ... My senses filled with an overwhelming awareness of the extraordinary contrast between the living, graceful, moving, young bodies before me and the old, dying body sitting next to me. An ocean of sadness and loss filled my being. Tears began to stream down my cheeks. The realization that I was confronting both my own past and future was quite sharp. My tears continued to wash my cheeks. My middle-aged body would never again move with the grace of the young dancers before me. It would most certainly move more and more toward the decay of the body sitting next to me. I allowed my tears their full measure."

Kathy, another class member, was eager to write about and explore her life. But she was afraid her topics were too ordinary and would not interest other people. During the quarter, she celebrated her fiftieth birthday. On that day, she was driving home in the middle of the afternoon and fell asleep at the wheel, going fifty miles an hour. Waking up, she found herself at the bottom of a steep hill in a demolished car, a few feet away from a telephone pole. She was unscathed but petrified. When she returned to look over the scene and her demolished car, she realized she was lucky to be alive. As she reflected, she came to view the experience as a call to honor her own experience as worthwhile material for her writing.

At a crucial point in my writing career, I chose to write poetry and fiction after having published journal articles and nonfiction books. I hit a wall, not in technique or content, but in an image of my deceased father standing in the middle of the road in front of me, blocking my path. I talked with a counselor to uncover what my father's discomfort was with my writing and found out that I believed he was threatened by my travels beyond his factual world. I had to let myself go past him in order to release my writing energy. I talked to him, telling him my feelings and asking for his support. With his support, I launched a new segment of my writing life.

Jack, a young man in class, wrote a long journal entry to his older brother, who was always better than he at everything they did. He poured out his anger and hurt in small script, but as he grew more courageous, he began to write in bolder, darker strokes. He told his brother how bad he felt in high school when he first started writing and his brother immediately got a poem published in the school literary review. In his journal, he asked his older brother to let him have his own style, and to support him when he asked. The older brother told him (in a dialogue in the journal) that he only tried to outshine him because he was also unsure of who he wanted to be. He surprised his younger brother by saying he would be glad to support him in his writing. The result was a passionate outflowing of stories, essays, and poems about teenage self-esteem.

Receiving the Angel's Gift

The second aspect of wrestling with our angel is being persistent and asking for what we deserve: a gift or blessing. Each time we wrestle with our angel, we receive another gift, more of our greatness, our passion, our courage to speak out, our identity as writers. Our angel has one goal, to help our writing take on its natural greatness. In granting the blessing, our angel encourages us to write courageously, to delve into forms, styles, content, and collaborations that we would have left untouched before. Another way to think of this is that each time we engage with our dark shadow we can go beyond that to our golden shadow, which is the angel's gift. I describe that process more thoroughly in Chapter 11, "Shadow and Writing."

As a result of wrestling with our angel, we begin to feel an intimacy with each piece of writing and understand where it is taking us. We listen to it, converse with it, wait when it is silent, write when it is urging us, take the sudden leaps of faith to which it invites us. We write what *compels* us, and in the form it requests of us. The results frequently surprise us. It is always an adventure. Although wrestling invariably involves insight or pain, it need not be a negative experience. Through the wrestling, we gain freedom we never knew before, not to mention more intimacy with ourselves and with the Holy, who is our source of the courage for the journey.

One woman, Karen, having engaged in an inner journey involving dreams, got an unexpected gift. She wrote a poem that led to a healing revelation and a significant conversation with her son. Reading this poem publicly took her to a new level of courage.

Lament

Walking in the moonlight
Wearing a victim's shawl
I carry a bucket of blood
It is my son's
I have it, extracted in payment
 for safety
His life for my safety
Behind the soothing screen of sentiment
 were horrors of shape-shifting anger
Terrors greater than his nightmares
Keening at the knowing, naked,
 skinned of denial
The knife light of compassion in my eyes
Bones licked clean in the flames of forgiveness

In writing classes, I lead a visualization exercise, inviting each person to go on a journey with their wisdom figure (a wise figure from history, religious tradition, or current life whom they trust) and receive a gift that is crucial and peculiar to their writing process. Polly followed her path and sat down on a bench in a wooded place near a rushing stream to meet her wisdom figure, who emerged from the woods and approached her, giving her a box containing a statue that represented reverence. The thought of reverencing her writing transformed her. She felt a calling to write about her life in a way that she had been afraid of before. She went on to write deeply moving memoirs.

Another writer, Scott, was strongly blocked in the middle of a novel. He had already published four books. He switched to journaling for a period of time and found strong, unresolved grief from deep childhood abuse he had suffered. With the help of a counselor, he stayed in that depressed and frightening place for several months until he felt some understanding and resolution of the pain. Out of the experience emerged immense compassion and a deepened spirituality. When he resumed his writing, he noticed immediately that his characters had taken on more depth than he had been capable of giving them before.

One small group of writers got together and decided to wrestle together and let their writing take them deeper. Their writing, though on varying topics of family, work, and relationships, took on a similar theme, grief and loss, but everyone was writing from different angles, within different forms. When they noticed the similarity, it was a sacred moment, and they treated the syncronicity with reverence. Peak experiences erupted in several members' lives.

After wrestling with my angel, I have come to view my writing much more broadly than before. It is as broad as my angel wants to make it. Now I write what I feel called to say, in whatever form or with whatever content it requires. That astounds and confuses me, because it messes up my neatly planned life of writing books on subjects I can also speak on to make a living. I am currently writing an article on how power is misused in the ministry, a book on domestic violence, a book on how suffering may increase our intimacy with God, and a fantasy about stars and black holes.

A Sacred Place in Your Life

The third aspect of wrestling with our angels is marking the spot— both internal and external—at which we touched our core and claimed our gift. We need to remember it as a sacred place. How often do we make sacred spaces in our life, places we can go back to and remember how we connected, where our sources of passion are, how we embraced our core, where we let our greatness emerge?

We can mark the spot in several ways. One internal way is to change our perspective: instead of seeing writing as a side venture, to see it as our core. This means letting writing have a sacred space in our lives. It means making a commitment to our writing because we have acknowledged it and accepted it as the gift it is. It may mean a shift in our priorities so that we set aside our best time for writing— even if it is for only one morning, or one day, a week—and find a way to work other things around it. Saving the best time for our writing allows our best to come out in our writing.

A writer with young children schedules day care every Monday morning so she can write early in the week, when she's refreshed. Her goal is to write one essay or letter to the editor every month, in addition to her other writing. In one year, she can write twelve essays instead of feeling bad that having small children precluded writing.

A full-time government employee whose passion is mystery writing uses Saturday mornings and his vacation time to write, taking one day every two to three weeks. He finished the first draft of his novel in fourteen months.

Symbols, pictures, phrases, and rituals also help reinforce the spirituality of our writing. Some people quiet down in reverence before they begin writing; they ask for writing guidance. Others light a candle or put on favorite music. I have six angels on my writing desk to remind me that I am on a journey. Taped to my computer is a picture of a statue representing the ancient story of Jacob wrestling with his angel; the statue is only one figure, half angel, half man. And I have a quote from the late Isaac Asimov, one of the most prolific and comprehensive writers of all time: "If I found out I had only ten minutes left to live, I'd just type faster."

So every time I enter my writing place, I remember that the place *from* which I write—my core—and the place *in* which I write are both sacred spaces. The visual reminders stay with me, so whenever I hesitate to write the more difficult thing, or I am tempted to take the easy way out in a piece, I will stop, see the visible reminder of the courageous way, and go for greatness and passion. I will let go of trying to control, trust the journey, and let the Holy speak. The reader can tell the difference.

Reflecting on the Chapter

1. Who or what first encouraged you in your writing? What effect did it have on you?

2. If you have recognized your angel, what is it like? What does it say to you?

3. Do you want to go deeper into your writing, into yourself? Why or why not?

4. Have you received your writing gift? What is it? How does if affect you?

5. How do you mark the spot of sacred writing in your life?

Writing Exercises

1. Have a dialogue in your journal with your angel. What does it say?

2. Describe how you got your gift from the angel, or how you think you will get it.

3. Write to the Holy, asking that you be shown how to wrestle with your angel. What is the response?

4. Write a short story which ends with the sentence, "I knew then that I would survive, that ..."

Visual Exercise

Draw yourself and your gift emerging from the wrestling match with your angel.

Guided Imagery

In your imagination, go to a warm and comfortable place and sit there surrounded by white light and peace. As you sit, you hear a rustling sound near you. You look and a form appears. It is your angel. Describe it. You and the angel begin wrestling. What form does that take for you? As you wrestle, you know it is a vital experience. You ask your angel for a blessing, a gift. The angel gives it to you. What is it? How do you feel? The angel quietly leaves and you rest. Slowly come back to the place of peace from which you started. Write about this experience in your journal.

TEN

≈

Dreams: A Pathway to the Soul

Dreams are the messengers of our souls. They are gifts from the Holy and want to be opened. They are friends who want us to be free, clear, and in close touch with our rich subconscious life. If we treat dreams with reverence and curiosity, we will get rich rewards, even if the dreams are difficult for us to remember or process.

Dreams have been around since the beginning of time and are recorded in many ancient texts. In the West, we are probably most familiar with those in the ancient Hebrew scripture. Jacob dreamed he saw a ladder joining earth and heaven, with angels walking up and down on it. Joseph interpreted the king's dream and became a court administrator. Daniel saved his own life, and other people's, by interpreting a king's dream and confronting him with it.

What do dreams have to do with writing? I believe if we listen to our dreams and find ways to enter their mysteries with reverence and expectation, they will bring us closer to our souls and to the core from which we write passionately. In *Dreams and Spiritual Growth*, Louis Savary, Patricia Berne, and Strephon Williams define soul as the dimension most directly connected to God. They call dreams the voice of the soul at work. Dreams are the area of activity where our ego and soul relate and cooperate.

Morton Kelsey, who writes about spirituality and the inner journey, says his dreams feel like a visit each night by someone who brings to his attention the things he needs to reckon with. He senses a wisdom in dreams that is greater than his rational mind. In *Sacrament of Sexuality,* he says of dreams, "I had heard about God speaking to human beings. I had read about it ... But here there was someone actually knocking at the door of my soul while I was sleeping. And the speech was in a universal language, trying to bring me to the Divine Lover."

Kelsey has been recording his dreams for over forty years, but he still remembers the first dreams that got his attention and helped him turn to dreams as a way of listening to his soul. "One night the presence of Dracula in a dream was so strong that I wondered if I should get up and put garlic on the windows just to be on the safe side. It was then I knew I should begin learning the meaning of my dreams."

Let's bring that down to a more practical level. What if you don't dream, or don't remember your dreams? What if you dream but don't know how to make sense of your dreams? And what does your dream life have to do with your writing life on a day-to-day basis? The answers to these questions vary. Research shows that everyone dreams but that not everyone remembers dreams. One approach I've used to remember dreams is to reverently ask my inner dream maker (perhaps my angel) and the Holy for dreams, and for the courage to look at them.

When dreams come and are particularly hard to understand, you can read books about dreaming or ask for help from someone who is educated in dream work. These people may be available at retreats or spiritual direction centers, or they may be professional clergypersons, counselors, or therapists.

At times in my life, I remembered dreams every night for months and felt that they were leading me along, on a daily basis, through difficult times. At other times, I don't remember more than snippets of dreams. And I have some vivid memories of wake-up dreams that are still as clear as when I dreamed them. Some of these wake-up dreams have changed my life and my writing.

I have categories for my dreams, some of which I created from experience and some of which I learned from reading books on dream work. I have life-change dreams, in which I am in a college setting— my symbol of a place of higher learning. Whenever I have a college dream, I know I am going through change and I become alert to the possibilities. I have warning dreams, in which an angry or dangerous person appears, trying to hurt me. I know something is askew and I need to be mindful of what is going on inside me and around me. Birth and baby dreams are signs of creativity and new life, which I need to nurture and support. Repeated dreams are signs that I am in a transition or am repeating an old pattern. And dreams that wake me up are signals I need to be attentive *now*. Many of my dreams are pedestrian dreams, which just process the activities of the day.

Dreams and Writing

How do we connect our dreams to our writing? Let Margaret tell her story: "One night in class, we discussed how to use our dreams to learn more about our writing. I have always worked with my dreams, but on an elementary level. What has happened to my dreaming process in relation to my writing since that night has been truly amazing. The night we talked about dreams, I read the class one of my short stories. On the way home, my critic was babbling in my ear, negative, negative, negative. That night I dreamed:

> I am with many people. There is a powerful, evil woman in our midst and we all live in fear of her because she can harm us, destroy us. I am standing high up on a beam of some kind, holding an infant. The fear of being harmed by her becomes so great I just decide to end it. I jump off the beam and hurl myself toward the ground with the child in my arms. I want to protect the child, too, and see that sparing the child the pain from this evil creature is acceptable and desirable. But the evil woman sees us fall and stops the fall somehow, letting us know we aren't going to get off that easily! Then the rest of the dream is me attempting to hide or go unnoticed by her—I keep trying to quiet the child, hugging her close. I think, "If we are quiet and she doesn't notice us, she won't hurt us."

Margaret wrote in her journal, "I know what the dream is about and it points to how powerful my critic is! I read a story out loud to my writing class last night and afterwards went through all my negative thoughts: It was boring, you took up too much of the class time, it was poorly written ... How powerful that negative voice is! If I'm just quiet and not noticed, I won't get hurt. If I don't take any risks, I won't feel any pain. But today I feel positive. I see the strength and power of my critic—I see it for what it is. It wants to stop me, hold me back. It is evil in its own way. And it is within me. My writing is like a small child I am nurturing and protecting. How willing I was to just throw in the towel to protect the child from further pain. Naming it is half the battle! I don't have a name but now I have a face—and a feeling—and a sense of the hold she wants to have over me and my budding interest in writing. And I will wrestle with her so that I can claim what is *mine!*"

In class, Margaret's biggest challenge was writing in a form she thought she wasn't capable of—short stories. Although she loved reading short stories, she was afraid she couldn't write one herself. She traced the fear back to her childhood. Up to about age thirteen, she wrote poetry, prose, and songs. After high school started, her creative side shut down. Her critic's message was, "Don't show off, don't take all the attention." So she only wrote in her journal from that time on—until coming to writing class at age forty-four.

For two weeks, she came to class and read from her journal or mentioned what she'd been thinking about when she hadn't written. Then in the third class, she confessed she'd written a short story but was afraid to read it. With encouragement, she read a poignant story about holidays in which alcohol addiction intruded and she was caught in the family system.

That night, Margaret dreamed her first infant dream. For the next several weeks, she dreamed infant dreams: adopted infants, abandoned infants, infants of different nationalities. In all the dreams, she was trying to keep and care for these babies. She concluded, "I knew that I was dreaming about my 'infant', my writing, and learning how to find, keep, own, nourish this small budding part of me. I looked forward to my nightly sleep, not knowing what new twist my dreams of infants would take!"

Learning From Dreams

How was it possible for Margaret to make sense of all these dreams and move beyond her understandable fear of the evil woman? She could have understood these dreams on many different levels. She could have concluded that the dream was telling her not to write— that scary women would come and get her if she did. She could have interpreted the evil woman as me, projecting her fear of writing onto me. To put the question more generally, how do we think about dreams so that they can give us another level of truth and take us to new places in our lives and our writing, while at the same time being truthful and not taking the energy out of the dream?

There are a myriad of ways to work with or interpret dreams. Freud was one of the first people to make a science out of dream interpretation. Although he may be controversial now, he did give the inner life public recognition. His approach to dreams was highly sexualized, which is probably related to the repressed Victorian era in which he lived. Jung's approach to dreams is metaphoric, which is appealing to me for its richness. Jungian analysts spend most of their therapeutic time working with their clients' dreams. To them, it is an art form. Many books suggest various ways to interpret dreams. I encourage you to trust yourself and your own insights about your dreams, and to augment your dream work with books if they interest you. There is no single right way.

I offer just one warning, based on what I have seen happen to some people who do dream work. Systems of dream symbols can be intriguing. You can look up every symbol in your dream to see what someone else says it means. That may be useful, but if you accept too many other people's interpretations of your dream, it ceases to be yours. Be willing to consider outside views, but remember to ask yourself, What does this symbol suggest to *me*? What does it remind me of? What significance does it have in my life? Remember, it is your dream, and what you take from it needs to be personal.

The following are the ways I make meaning of my dreams. I learned them from three wise women who each approach the process a little differently. I will use a turning point dream to illustrate my process.

Pray into the dream and ask for guidance

Ask to see clearly, to be safe, and to use the messages of the dream as messages from the Holy and from your soul.

Record the dream in first person

Write the dream down as soon as possible (especially if you wake up in the middle of the night), before you forget any segments. You will be surprised how quickly dreams flee.

Let's take a dream of mine to work with:

> The King of Egypt, a playboy, is in the United States cavorting, going to school, fooling around. He comes to his senses, realizes he is addicted and is wasting his life. He decides to finish school—only one more semester—and then commit to building adequate housing for everyone in Egypt, overseeing it himself. He is living in shoddy housing that he initiated and built. I am aware I do not need to be involved with him in his old ways. I am attracted to the thrill of his cavorting but I am also aware that I can know this new person and respect him.

Underline the important words, images or feelings in the dream

You may want to do this and you may not, depending on how potent the dream is. If you do, it will help you with the next step.

My dream underlining: king, Egypt, cavorting, school, senses, addicted, wasting, finish, commit, everyone, overseeing, shoddy housing, initiated, aware, old ways, attracted, thrill, know, respect.

Trace the feeling progression of the dream

You, the dreamer, are sometimes aware of your feelings during the dream. Name the feelings and the progression of feelings that you are not immediately aware of as well, because they will give you added insights. This means going back over the dream and asking what feelings you are having as you reread the dream.

In my dream, I am aware of shameful feelings about the king's behavior. Then I feel fear around the addictions and the possible behavior they could stimulate. Next I am aware of feeling some relief when he comes to his senses and sees that he is wasting his life and can turn it around. The last feeling I have is a combination of calm and courage. This feeling progression is characteristic of me: first fear or shame, then if an insight comes, relief. Usually this is followed by calm, or by a feeling of being able to live anew.

Dreams can sometimes point us to feeling progressions in our lives that we have not been aware of but which can help us find inner wisdom.

Find yourself in the dream

Make each figure and image of the dream a part of yourself so you can personalize the dream and drop down to the subtle messages it may have for you. Literal interpretations are interesting, but hardly ever lead you to the significant messages. This requires that you be honest with yourself, sometimes painfully honest, asking the dream and the Holy to reveal you to yourself.

Try assuming that masculine figures are the masculine side of you, (regardless of your gender), feminine figures are the feminine side, and figures you know represent the part of you that is like them. For people you recognize in dreams, list three characteristics that describe them and apply those traits to yourself. Here is my interpretation of my dream:

My arrogant, danger-loving masculine—especially present when I am in an insecure time of life—has been away from home, reveling in a foreign place. My real home is close to my roots, my own inner culture, an ancient culture, my cradle of civilization. Now is the time for my masculine to take a serious turn and give up the front he has kept up. It is time to finish school, my inner learning, my higher learning. I need to work on meaningful, life-long projects, and be aware that too much energy has been going to my addictions or to false or empty achievements. These last six years in "college" (deep learning and counseling) have taught me to spend my life on building "structures" (ideas, programs, relationships, causes) that last, that make a difference for me and other people, that adequately "house" us and our souls.

Relate the dream to something in your current life experience

You can do this after you personalize the dream figures and objects, or you can do it while you are personalizing the dream. In this case, I integrated it, so I will proceed with my dream and you can see how it relates to my current life:

The soul structures that last for me are domestic violence reduction programs, writing, soul writing classes and books, spiritual direction, supportive teaching, loving husband, family and friends, encouraging people to try new possibilities, journeying with women in prison. I will have to personally oversee the "building" so I am sure it is well done. I am more likely to produce shoddy structures if I am in a hurry and don't take time to be thoughtful. And I will stay with my calling, even in hard, slow, or unsuccessful times. Now I am committed to a more in-depth life, building adequate soul structures for me and others.

The grounded feminine in me does not have to be attracted to this old kind of fast-tracker or ride his coattails. I am attracted to my own new, masculine depth, my reflective inner place, my willingness to work in healthy ways for everyone, not just a few people. I can be whole, aware of myself, and respectful of myself. Amen. What a remarkable dream. Thank you.

My dream contained only one person, some buildings, and my own ego. Other dreams have many people and objects, which complicate them. Pick the things that stand out for you, and work with them. Keep asking yourself, what does this mean to me? What association do I make with this symbol?

Dialogue with the dream characters

If you're not clear about a dream, talk to its figures or images and let them answer you, writing down what you both said in your journal. If I had been less clear about the king of Egypt, I would have done this. He might have told me the same things I learned myself or he might have come up with new material.

Ponder the meaning of the messages for you and name the dream

Our dreams frequently hold messages that benefit us if we can receive them. Ask what message your dream carries. My dream was an important dream for me because it came when I was wondering how much time to devote to my writing, how much to other work, and how much to volunteer activities. The dream told me to devote time to whatever deepens and builds solid structures. It gave me a standard by which to measure whether the things I do in my life are worthwhile. The title I gave it was "Soul Building." Now I ask myself, no matter what I am engaged in, is it soul building? And I know, deep within myself, whether or not it is. If it isn't, I find a way to discontinue it. This dream pointed me in a new direction, one I had been searching for, but had not yet clearly found until this dream announced it.

Consider what question the dream is asking of you

If you don't have the time to go into a dream as deeply as you would like, ask yourself what question it poses.

The question my dream asked was, "Do you have the courage to live out this soul building mission to your fullest?"

Margaret had a dream at the end of class that may take her to a new place in her life:

> I was standing in a beautiful river fly fishing. I have never been fly fishing in my life, but I was really enjoying this, casting the thin line out over and over again. I thought, "Wow! I could really develop a touch for this." I spotted a fish in the water and cast my line for it. It moved closer to me, and as it did, I realized that it wasn't a fish—it was an alligator. I stumbled toward the river bank in fear, with weak and heavy legs.
>
> I struggled out of the river and entered a cabin that was high on stilts. I walked out on a large deck that overlooked the river and saw something huge in the water. As I peered over the railing into the river, I realized that it was a huge perch, about ten feet long. And then I saw more and more of these huge fish slowly swimming just beneath the surface.

She interprets: "The alligator portion of this dream told me that I still have considerable fear about trying to be a writer and about searching for my voice. As I 'fish' for my stories, it can be scary, especially when I come up blank, or what I thought was a good idea feels flat on paper. But having a little more distance (the cabin on stilts) keeps me safe. From this vantage point, I know that just below the surface I am holding some powerful stories about everyday life. They are slowly swimming, down in my subconscious. I can barely see them, but I am willing to continue to work and explore."

Margaret's summary of her writing class experience is this: "I realized that I need a lot of support to keep on writing ... My mother told me as a young girl that if I wanted to be a writer, I would be *writing*. Writers write ... Now I know that not all writers write! I was a writer who, for many reasons, was not writing ... I also learned to write what *I* wanted, not what I thought I should be writing. I learned that I can't force myself to write in a style or length with which I am not comfortable. I learned to explore this entire process by writing about it. When I am struggling now, I write about struggling. When I am stuck, I write about being stuck. But, most of all, I just keep writing."

Dreams allow us to make a connection with a part of ourselves that is ordinarily inaccessible. They allow our soul to make a connection with the Holy. Dreams may come to encourage us, warn us, educate us, deepen us. They give us guidance for our life and our writing.

Reflecting on the Chapter

1. Do you record and remember dreams? If not, try asking your dream maker and the Holy to bring you a dream. Record your remembered dream here.

2. What are the important repeating symbols in your dreams?

3. How do your dreams affect your writing journey?

4. What is your most effective way of working on dreams? Looking back at your learning style might help you with this.

5. How can you honor and trust dreams more in your life?

Writing Exercises

1. Make up a dream you would like to have. Write it out.

2. The object or symbol that most encourages me to dream is ...

3. A birth dream would indicate to me ...

4. A death dream would indicate to me ...

5. What question is this chapter asking of me?

Visual Exercise

Draw a key symbol, word, or idea from a turning point dream, or from another important dream of yours. What does it mean to you?

Visualization

Quietly go to the place inside you where the dream maker makes dreams. Imagine that inner space as a garden. Watch the Holy and your dream maker as they pick dreams off bushes, flower patches, rose bushes, and trees for you. Smell the fragrance, hear the sounds, feel the warmth of the environment. Feel yourself relaxed, expectant, and satisfied that they know what is best for you. Return to your present environment and write about the experience.

ELEVEN

Shadows and Writing

An ancient story goes like this:

> A king had been off to war and was now returning to his castle. As he approached the last turn in the road on his way home, his dog could sense his homecoming and ran out to meet him. This was his beloved dog, whom he had left at home to guard his baby and the castle. He trusted the dog more than anything else in the world and they had been companions for years.
>
> The king noticed the dog was highly agitated and had blood all around his mouth. He knew instantly that something was wrong. The dog barked and ran toward the castle.
>
> When the king arrived at home, the halls were smeared with blood. He was terrified, for his baby was in this wing of the castle. The dog ran toward the baby's room. When the king entered the room he saw the baby's crib overturned and he heard no sounds. Enraged, he took out his sword and killed his beloved dog.
>
> Whimpering cries came from under the crib. The king turned the crib over and saw his baby with a dead wolf next to it. He took the baby in his arms and then realized what had happened. The wolf had gotten into the castle and his beloved dog had saved the life of his son. He held his son to his heart and wept with grief.

Clarissa Pinkola Estés tells this story in her audio tape "The Creative Fire" to help us understand the creative process and the ways we sabotage it. She says we need to protect our babies, our newly found creativity, and identify who our interior wolf is.

We can think of the wolf as our critic, bent on destroying our writing, our baby, this newly found creativity we want to develop. We can think of the faithful dog as our angel, trying to protect and nurture us, no matter what the cost.

The figure who most intrigues me is the king, the master, the psyche in the story. He has a powerful and loving relationship with his dog, his angel, and yet in a time of grief and panic, he kills the thing that is most faithful to him. His actions suggest that something bleak overcame him in his grief and he did the thing he hated most. As a writer, I can relate to that. Just when I'm on a roll, I have a tough time with a relationship, or I get bad news in some other part of my life, and what do I do? I kill my writing. I stop and let myself get blocked. Not because I don't have anything to write. In fact, I might have the first draft of a book finished. What is this mysterious power that overtakes me? What was the darkness that overcame the king and why did it have so much power?

Our Shadow

Shadow behavior shows up most strongly when we have experienced the deep urge to write and know, somewhere deep inside, that we can do it. This is more than a voice from our past saying we can't write, or that our writing is stupid. Those are external forces. This shadow comes from deep within ourselves. It is the inner, dark power of the king, who in the end has a dead wolf, a dead dog, and a frightened baby on his hands. Unless this shadow part is integrated, it will haunt us for the rest of our days. But once acknowledged and befriended, it can transform us and our writing.

The shadow has an equally strong and positive side, but that comes out only after we work with the negative shadow. The golden shadow is your angel's gift. They are inextricably connected to one another.

The psychiatrist Carl Jung first described the shadow and said that discovering and integrating it was part of the mid-life process. Shadow is that great reservoir of possibilities in our hidden selves, largely unknown to us and very private. In *Your Golden Shadow,* William Miller coins the term golden shadow and describes it as "an unconscious force within us—a source of power and possibility that we can bring into consciousness and use creatively and constructively for a fuller and more enriching experience of life."

Miller cites five ways to learn about our shadow: soliciting feedback from others, uncovering the content of our projections, examining our slips of tongue and behavior, considering our humor and identifications, and studying our dreams. We will consider one of these five ways, projections, because although it is disconcerting, it is also easiest to identify.

Think of several people you don't like or don't get along with. On the left hand side of this page, list the specific qualities you don't like about them. On the right hand side, in capital letters, list the qualities from the first list that you find despicable.

Negative Qualities   Despicable Qualities

_____   _____
_____   _____
_____   _____
_____   _____

The qualities you capitalized are your negative shadow, the things about yourself that you don't see.

To find the positive aspects of your shadow, just reverse the exercise. Think of several people you respect or admire. They can be alive or dead, famous or unknown. On the left list the qualities you like about them. Next, in capital letters, list the qualities you absolutely covet. These are the positive parts of your shadow which you have not yet developed, the potential gifts from your angel.

Positive Qualities   Outstanding Qualities

_____   _____
_____   _____
_____   _____
_____   _____

Both of these exercises are hard, because we want to deny both our negative traits and our positive ones, lest we have to embrace them and become whole. Before we talk about what to do to embrace them, let's examine shadow more thoroughly.

How can you identify your shadow in your writing life? Two ways come to mind. One is to do the exercise on negative shadow and see how the despicable qualities relate to your writing. For example, Kathleen despised high risk takers who put others in jeopardy. As she reflected on how that applied to her writing, she recalled three risky things she had done recently in her writing: stopped writing about nature and the environment, switched to fiction, and started writing only in a library. Yet she was stuck and feeling numb inside. Why had she made these changes? Because she read in a writing book that serious writers wrote only fiction with historical significance. By following this advice, her joy in writing disappeared. The person in jeopardy was herself.

At an even deeper level than that truth, she started to look at how she had let other people's opinions distract her throughout her life. Whenever she started moving in the direction of her heart, she would bump into a strong personality who had a different opinion. She had a pattern of letting other people determine her direction, and she was constantly in jeopardy.

Another way to relate shadow to writing is to look back at your writing and see what shadow emerges. For instance, if you sit down to write and you are afraid of what people will think of you if you write what you are thinking, you might look at abandonment issues in your shadow. If your fiction is made up of tough, harsh, independent characters who spend their time abusing other people, you might check out whether abuse is on your list of despicable characteristics, whether you are or were abused, or whether you abuse or have abused others. If your characters are meek, submissive, and passive, look at that cluster of traits in the recesses of your psyche. If you are caught with words in your throat but cannot get them out for fear of a gush of emotion, you might look at deep, unresolved grief in your past. If you are consistently angry in your writing, no matter what the form, you might look into your shadow for deep hurt.

Shadows, both negative and positive, are related to our persona. Miller says our persona is our outer personality—the part of ourselves that we show to the world. It allows us to function successfully, and we learned it in childhood. It consists of those behaviors that were acceptable to our family, our environment, our peers. We learned them well, and they have served us faithfully for many years.

One of the difficulties in understanding shadow is that our persona is largely unaware of it. The thicker our persona, the more massive our shadow. In other words, the more strictly or rigidly socialized we were, the stronger our shadow is. Shadow is every bit as strong as persona but opposite in character. And the end result of living out our persona without understanding shadow is inauthenticity and artificiality.

Both shadow and persona contain positive things, which we like about ourselves and negative things, which we don't like. Each positive part of our persona is related to an equal and negative part of our shadow, and vice versa. In order to become whole, we must integrate our shadow, not eliminate it. It is amazing to discover our shadow, but our resistance makes it hard to deal with it. Integrating it means coming to know it and understanding what it has to teach us.

The most distressing thing about shadow material is that we must encounter the things we don't like in our shadow before we can approach and redeem its golden aspects. Again, the task is not to get rid of its negative qualities, but to learn to appreciate them because of what they teach us about our wholeness. It is to accept them for what they are without having to act them all out.

Miller says that self-acceptance (accepting our shadow as well as our persona) is fundamental to self-development. Self-esteem is based on our ability to accept ourselves in our weaknesses as well as in our strengths.

Self-esteem is not related to our net worth or the number of people we supervise, or our title, or our travels, or even our activities. Self-esteem is based on self-acceptance, and that requires self-knowledge.

Uncovering these new areas in ourselves means acknowledging fear, uncertainty, ambiguity, pain. It means leaning into that fear, going ahead, even though it may be difficult. It means not knowing; waiting, sometimes patiently; and getting professional as well as holy guidance.

Things may even get worse before they get better. They frequently do as we heal. Believing that this is a healing journey, and that the Holy is at the base of that health, gives us the courage to go on. Then, with support and encouragement, the memories, pain, rage, understanding, compassion, and healing come.

Kathleen, the woman who let other people's opinions change what she wrote, found that behavior stifling to her real creativity. She did some long, hard thinking and talking about the early patterns of her life, living with strong mother and father figures who shaped her into their image of what they wanted her to be, not into who she was. Once she realized this truth, she returned to writing about nature and the environment in essays and children's fiction. She got the worst strep throat she had ever had and was in bed for four days.

She called on her writing angels and on the Holy during her illness. In her journal, she wrote about how her throat was closing up because of the fear of disobeying family rules. She got strong messages that she needed to love her throat and help it not be afraid to speak. As she recovered, she talked to her throat, promising to keep it safe, healthy, and informed. And she kept writing what she felt called to write.

Dale found out through the despicable qualities exercise and some feedback from an associate that he was intellectually arrogant. He thought he was above others in his writing and had nothing to learn from anyone. It bothered him. The real surprise for him was learning that arrogance is really a well-covered form of insecurity—not strength or superiority. Where did that leave him? Feeling worse than he had when he only knew he was arrogant. After all, he came by that honestly. His father was one of the most arrogant people he knew, and he hated that in him.

In talking this confusion over with a trusted friend who had been through a great deal of soul-searching and counseling, he realized that some deeper learning lay in this knowledge. His arrogance was a signal from his soul that there was something in the situation that he was afraid to learn. That's what his arrogance was trying to cover up. He was an excellent writer but was stuck because he was afraid to learn from others, especially those who had fewer publications than he.

Now he uses his arrogance as a signal to bring his awareness to a new level. Whenever he feels arrogant, he asks himself, "What am I afraid to learn from this person or situation?" His arrogance had become his teacher.

On the other side of his arrogance is a curious, open, vulnerable child who wants to learn, be taken care of, investigate. But only through the awareness of the shadow is that other side allowed to re-emerge and be supported.

If the negative shadow trait on your despicable list does not resonate with you at first, you may find the opposite behavior operating in yourself. Drivenness may be a fear of slowing down or of not accomplishing things; naivete may be an unwillingness to take responsibility for knowing things.

The same may be true of positive shadow traits. If you admire calmness under stress, but can't identify with it, you probably have a calm reservoir that wants to be discovered.

Sickness of the Soul

At mid-life particularly, the shadow, the hidden parts of us, beg to be uncovered and incorporated into our lives. This is why changing forms or trying a new desk may not solve the problems we have to solve. Surface changes will never solve shadow issues. In fact they may exacerbate them—which is what some of us need in order to see them clearly.

In our struggle to find what is right for our lives, we may try taking classes, writing faster, going to readings, taking writing trips. None of these work for long. We are really facing a block inside, which it is imperative to break through. We need a transformation. We need a death and rebirth. But we're feeling insecure and afraid and covering it with verve, and sometimes even with arrogance.

In *Walking on Water,* Madeleine L'Engle says of the spiritual process of writing that we die to self in order to become a servant of the work. "We move—are moved—into death in order to be discovered, to be loved into truer life by our Maker. To die to self in the prayer of contemplation is to move to a meeting of lovers ... That is our Calling, the Calling of all of us, but perhaps it is simplest for the artist ... to understand, for nothing is created without this terrible entering into death."

Miller says being stuck is a "sickness of the soul; it is a matter concerning one's whole being."

It helps to find or renew our spiritual selves on this inner journey. This frequently requires that we get outside support and help: from professional counselors, spiritual directors, or wise older writers who've been through the shadows. They can give us the added courage and support we need to probe more deeply and they can help us see this as a sacred time in our lives, even though we are vulnerable. I write about this in Chapter 13, on writers' spiritual issues.

Golden Shadow

The golden shadow represents the writer inside, who wants to develop into a humorist, a storyteller, a journalist—whatever.

Leatha achieved success at a young age against many odds. She was an African-American who grew up in the South and received a master's in creative writing when many of the young women she grew up with hadn't finished high school. She published widely and taught part-time at a university. But in her late thirties she plateaued, and she couldn't figure out why. She tried everything—changing her hair, her clothes, her relationships with men. She even had an unexpected surgery that allowed her time to think things over in some depth. Finally she began seeing snapshots of her family in her dreams and in waking reflective moments. The snapshots were all about abuse.

She faced that truth and got professional help. During her therapy, an urge grew from within her to begin taking photographs. How ironic, since her pain emerged from photos in her mind.

Her interest and ability grew. Her mind framed images and she went out to find them. The same ability that showed her painful truth showed her brilliant beauty and poignant scenes. She began doing photographic essays on the South. The project transformed her writing and her professional career and brought joy to her life.

Inside all of us is a wonderful creative writer who desperately wants to emerge and to speak to the world. The scary part is finding out who and where that writer is.

Some people look at the things they listed in their golden shadow list and laugh. They think they could never do or be those things. A courageous leader? A world changer? It seems ridiculous, far fetched. Let's say you wrote down athletic and wise as two of your most admired traits. It means something inside is drawing you to those traits.

You may never be athletic like a twenty-year old olympic runner, but your body may want to be in better shape. And you can always write about athletes if your heart is drawn there. Wisdom may not be easy to achieve, but you could write about wise people, try to sprinkle your fiction or poems with wisdom, or go on a deliberate spiritual journey to discover wisdom in yourself or others.

When we begin to acknowledge our golden shadow—our gifts—we begin writing from a strong sense of interior freedom and we uncover the deepest desires of our heart. It is a transformation of mammoth proportions.

I admire people who have survived great pain and turned that into service to the world. Persistence, courage, and joy are deeply satisfying to my soul. During my darkest years, I wrote into the darkness rather than remain silent. I wrote about death and I wrote about healing, both of which I needed to own in my own psyche.

After my journey into my own darkness I discovered the deep calm and courage of being a survivor and the healing power of telling my story more clearly in my writing. I find I have more compassion and understanding and my story empowers others and gives them hope—living hope. And I find that I am not afraid of writing about difficult truths, about critics and angels and suffering. I feel more joy than I have ever known.

Your golden shadow is what your angel gives you when the wrestling is over. It is your gift, your freedom, your deepest heart's desire. It is a gift from the Holy, and only by going into the dark shadow and sitting there at the Holy's feet in reverence of life and of the process of healing does the gift appear.

What would have happened in the story of the king, the baby, the dog, and the wolf if the king had come into the room and let the feelings of grief and rage come over him, sitting down on the floor and weeping about the futility of it all? What if he could have called for help, or let compassion flood in, by lifting the baby or turning over the cradle before he let his shadow rage control him? What if he could have seen the wolf and gotten the baby to safety and then wept for the dog and held the dog in his arms and thanked him from the bottom of his grief and fear? How might he and the dog and the baby have been different? How might our lives and our writing be different if we had the courage to face and embrace our dark and golden shadows?

Reflecting on the Chapter

1. How is the Holy calling you to a deeper place?

2. What is your most prevalent dark shadow characteristic? What does it mean to you?

3. What is your most prevalent golden shadow? What does this mean to you?

4. What is the most vulnerable spot in your writing process?

5. What will you do with your gift?

Writing Exercises

1. Write to your dog, your wolf, your baby, your king.

2. What I regret most in my life is ...

3. What's become clear to me about my writing is ...

Visual Exercise

Draw your dark shadow by giving it a symbol, color, texture, or name. Do the same with your golden shadow.

Guided Imagery

Tape the story of the king, dog, wolf, and baby. Find a safe, quiet place to listen to it. As you play it, visualize the story in your mind and imagine yourself as one of the characters. Which is it? Write about how that resonates in you and what you can do to heal that character in you.

TWELVE

Receiving the Angel's Gift

Our angel has one goal, to help our writing take on its natural greatness. Each time we wrestle with our angel, each time we face our shadows or blocks, we receive a gift or blessing: more of our greatness, our passion, our courage to speak out, our identity as writers. And we get a new name, a new image as writers, just as Jacob, the ancient angel-wrestler did. This process is about intimacy with ourselves, with the Holy, and with our writing. It is the most satisfying and energizing process imaginable.

One of my students, Anne, wrote about a powerful gift story she received along her spiritual journey. I pass this gift along to you.

> The idea for my story "Pine Lands" came to me about midnight one night. I never fall asleep easily, and this night was no exception. Most of my published work had been nonfiction, or fiction based on historical facts. My imagination could run only within the parameters of the facts. As I lay there, I thought of some of the fiction I had recently read and decided to attempt that kind of writing. It had to be something I already knew, something I had somehow lived. Then the idea came. Each year, when my family goes to a resort in northern Minnesota with another family, I enjoy speculating on what it would be like to stay there and live in an isolated, northern area all winter.
>
> So what would happen if someone did that? I gave it enough thought to assure myself that I would remember it tomorrow and I went to sleep.
>
> The next morning, after my kids were off to school, I sat down at my computer and began to type. No notes, no rough drafts on paper, no struggle with an opening paragraph. It was as if the

story were already there. I had only to put my fingers to the keyboard and let my imagination run.

And it ran, with no stumbles, no hesitation, day after day. Never had writing come so easily.

Each day as I worked, I got so immersed in the story that my surroundings receded. I felt the northern woods surrounding me. If the phone rang, I was startled. It took me a few moments to focus on the person calling, as if I had to leave my story's setting first.

I worked in the mornings, and then the daily hubbub of family life took over. At night, before I slept, I was reading a book called *Where Angels Walk*. It was the second book of angel stories that I had read in the past few months. They were fascinating stories, uplifting and hopeful.

My story was progressing. Ideas unfolded and worked together perfectly. Soon I knew that somehow an angel must appear in the story. I wrote that character in as I did the other ideas: The time was right, the idea was there.

He entered the story slowly, appropriately, then did his important task, and left. It was not difficult to write.

I wrote the whole story in about three weeks. Ideas for the upcoming sections sometimes came when it was inconvenient to write, but I had come to understand the way of this story. I stopped what I was doing to write down the ideas. Sometimes I abandoned what I had been doing altogether and turned on the computer. That story called to me, I guess.

I was amazed at how little revision I needed to do. There were no unclear parts. And then there are the symbols: things I wrote in the first part that later became symbols; foreshadowing I planned that worked easily; foreshadowing I didn't plan and was startled by when I reread it; themes that a friend found which I had not only not done consciously, but had not seen at all.

Receiving the Gift

How do we make ourselves available to receive these gifts? The wrestling process is the stimulus we can use to get started. It asks us to look directly at fear and find out what we are afraid of.

With support from friends and from the Holy, we can face that fear and unleash the power that has been trapped inside the fear, using that power to fuel our passion. The power of fear and passion come from the same core place in us, and unless we go there slowly and with courage, we will have a difficult time breaking through to great writing. The angel's gift to us involves passion, freedom, and courage.

I know of four ways to open ourselves to the angel's gift while facing our shadow: use of imagery; finding intimacy with our writing; prayer; and working with our spiritual issues. I write at length about the spiritual issues in the next chapter, so I will focus on the other three here.

Imagery

A wonderful way of using our imagination to help us receive the angel's gift is to deliberately quiet down and invite the Holy to bring images to our imagination. To do this, ask for symbols or images to come into your mind which have specific meaning for you and for your writing. Trust that the Holy will give you life-giving imagery, even if the images are difficult to accept.

Once I asked for an image of what my writing represented and the Holy gave me the image of a woman sitting on a chair with her hands tied behind her back. When I wrote about that image in my journal, it became clear that I was feeling stuck, and in danger of some kind. It scared me into action. I took a series of writing courses to stimulate me and give me new direction. The image I have for my writing now is that I am soaring on eagle's wings. What a difference. Yet if I hadn't listened to the early image, I might still be sitting there with my hands tied behind my back.

If you are not used to asking for images, or if you do not create images easily, you might try thinking of your mind as a motion picture screen on which the image, symbol, or story will appear. Don't worry if no image comes; it may not be your method of learning.

If images do come to you, try the following guided imagery. You may want to tape it, using a gentle, soothing voice, then sit quietly and listen to the tape so you can take full advantage of your experience. Remember to start the experience by asking for the Holy to accompany you, making this a safe and private experience.

> I welcome you to this journey to your soul, and to the gift the Holy has for you and your writing. Begin by being quiet, letting your breathing be slow and natural ... Breathe in ... Breathe out ... Relax and let each part of your body rest as you move with your mind through each part. Experience a sacred, warm, white light surrounding you. The light is safe and nurturing.

Go in your imagination to a safe and nourishing place that you have been to or that you can imagine. Be aware of that environment—what is there, who is there, what surrounds you. What are the smells, sights, colors, textures around you? Are you outside or inside? What is the weather like? Just be in that environment for a safe time. (Pause)

Now imagine that a wisdom figure is sent by the Holy to guide you on a journey. What does the figure look like, act like, feel like to you? (Pause) The wisdom figure takes you on a walk down a meandering path through lush woods that border a cool, rushing stream filled with sunken rocks and foaming eddies. You continue to walk until you come to an opening in the trees and you see an inviting bench. It is time for a rest. As you rest, the wisdom figure looks behind you and notices a presence emerging from the woods. You look and notice an angel coming toward you. What are your reactions to the presence of the angel as it approaches?

The angel stops next to the bench and gazes at you lovingly. How does its face seem to you? It hands you a box with your name on it. What size is the box? How is it wrapped? How do you respond? (Pause) Slowly you open the box and reveal its contents. It is especially for you and represents a gift from your angel for your writing. What is your gift? What significance does it have for you? If you do not know the significance, just name the gift and be aware of the gratefulness in your heart for this wonderful gift. Sit with the gift and let whatever feelings you have emerge. (Pause)

As the angel moves slowly away be aware of the awe of this moment, this visitation of the Holy representative to your writing. Bask in gratefulness. Be aware that you are safe and that your wisdom figure is there beside you. When you are ready, walk back down the path and slowly back into the scene you first placed yourself in when the wisdom figure appeared. Sit quietly until you are ready to re-enter your present world. Be aware of your breathing and the sacredness of this experience. Write about the experience and the gift in your journal. Discuss it with friends, writers, or a spiritual director when it is comfortable for you.

Students have received various gifts from this experience, and many of them have caused a change in direction, affirmed a project, or guided a writer into a new era. I have received book concepts in imageries like this one. They seem to arrive already packaged and all I need to do is unwrap them. One student was given her whole writing future by the jewel she received. Another received a yardstick and realized she was measuring all of her writing by what she thought about other people's writing. Her yardstick had no numbers on it, so it was almost impossible to measure her work precisely any more. She decided to use the yardstick as a flagpole and make up her own flag of independence from the tyranny of comparisons.

Intimacy With Your Writing

This concept will sound crazy to some people, but many writers form relationships with their writing so they can listen and speak back and forth with it. This is yet another way to receive the gift the angel wants to give us. It can be disconcerting, because we just don't know what we will find out when we enter into the relationship. And it takes courage, because our egos are involved and our minds think they know more than our souls.

Sometimes writers sit down with an agenda and try hard to write but find it hard because some other piece wants to emerge. Or they take on whole projects that are not a labor of love, but a struggle with endurance. If these writers would ask the writing what is going on, they might hear that the piece that wants to emerge is more important than the one they're committed to. I frequently ask my writing who is most interested in working with me that day and go with whoever speaks up. Sound strange? If I don't go with that voice, I end up spending twice as much time as I had planned working on the piece I chose. Sometimes I have to write a poem or an essay before my mind is clear enough to go ahead.

I have a friend who has been ghostwriting for years and is finding it more laborious than before, even though she is better at it. Each chapter is a struggle that brings her little satisfaction when it is finished. Last year, she wrote her first book with her own name on it. What a difference. Such joy, such satisfaction, even though the amount of work was about equal. She is beginning to see that her writing is telling her to write her own work, even if that means facing fears and financial difficulties. She sees it as a faith journey, trusting the Holy enough to take her where she needs to go.

Prayer and Contemplation

I cannot overestimate the power of prayer and contemplation in the spiritual life of writers. Prayer is a conscious relationship with the Holy. It involves becoming intimate with this power and working from the level of daily conversation, sacred struggle, and conscious faithfulness to our calling in writing. Some people are more comfortable with the words meditation or contemplation, although they have different connotations for different people. I am talking about prayer in two ways: as a way of quieting down and centering, and as a way of being deliberately in the presence of and in an intimate relationship with the Holy.

Although there are well over twenty forms of prayer, I suggest you take some time every day to quiet down and get to know the Holy if you are interested in receiving the gift of the wrestling process. This is not easy and it does not come naturally in our hurried world. Some people cannot imagine sitting still for even ten minutes without reading mail or watching TV. Others see prayer as a sign of weakness, a dependency on someone other than yourself. It's helpful to be aware of these reactions, because they form the core of your resistance to the Holy and will help you find out what your inner work is.

One of my writer friends, after participating in a domestic violence exhibit project, and after doing some of her own inner work, started receiving a powerful image related to a rape she had survived ten years earlier but had not written about. She went to her journal and the words began pouring out of her. She just let them come. As she tapped into her unresolved grief, a vision of a book came to her. But between herself and the book, was a boulder. She said, "I tried to go around it for months. Then I pretended it was not there. I tried leaping over it—just forging ahead, but that didn't work either. Finally I realized I couldn't go forward without dealing with the boulder—me."

During that same period, she dreamed of a huge and powerful male angel in the sky. The angel yelled at her, "Are you awake?" She got irritated with the angel and said, "Yes, I'm awake." The angel said, "Okay," and threw a book down to her. She was filled with delight. At last. She had the answer. On the cover of the book were a line drawing and a title, *The Tree*, but when she opened it, it was empty. She realized that she was to fill the book. She is still waiting to understand the significance of the title, but she decided to take a risk and start writing a book on rape, even though memoir is a new form for her.

Many people have trouble deciding what to pray for and wonder, when they do perceive guidance, whether it is the Holy or their own ego speaking to them. I have found after reading, and after observing myself and those I work with, that the more we trust the Holy, the more we can pray for general rather than specific things. Many people ask for a certain job, or a mate, or a contract. If they get it, the Holy is good. If they don't, the Holy is at fault—or worse yet, punishing them. I have also seen people whose trust and image of the Holy has changed so much over time that they can pray for strength, courage, and peace, no matter what happens in their lives, trusting that the Holy will be there in each of life's events, showing them the way to greater intimacy and growth, even in pain. I often remind people of the old saying, "Be careful what you pray for. You may get it." Lucy, of "Peanuts" fame, went to her bed and knelt beside it, only to get up right away and go back into the kitchen. She said to Charlie Brown, "I was praying for patience and tolerance, but I quit. I was afraid I might get it."

A good way to begin praying is to sit quietly, walk, or be in nature for ten minutes a day, asking the Holy to be close to you, to show you the path on which you are to go, and to accompany you along the way. Then if you should come upon a frightening or challenging experience—say a burning bush—you will know you are not alone and that even though the bush is burning, you are on holy ground. If you cannot imagine talking to or being close to the Holy, first read Chapter 13, on the spiritual issues of writers.

A student of mine, Charles, wrote this about his emerging prayer life.

> Noise, then silence, then noise in my head. Or is it my heart and I just hear it in my head? What do raindrops find when they pass inside the earth's dark interior? After a few days I got used to the little voices and figured they were demanding to be heard at this time each morning. After all, they've been getting cheated for years. Oh, they'd been in my life, but they had to sneak in. And I've learned from them. Now they have an official audience so they can participate in my living and my writing. This was definitely good. I knew that I only needed patience and some part of my interior would become visible.

I went to my next spiritual direction meeting and reported, like a proud third grader, that my assignment was done. "Beginning," I was reminded. Ten minutes cautiously grew to fifteen each morning, first thing, before I'm drawn through a one-way door out of quiet, where I would remain until I slept again. Now I began this prayer time with no expectations, so it was a surprise that within two weeks a great void was revealed to me. The name is affiliation.

How do we make sense of the direction, voice, or images we are getting? Whose are they? Ours or the Holy's? Here are some questions you can ask to test out what is from the Holy.

- What will this insight or suggestion do to my ego? Mature it or inflate it?
- Would I have thought of this myself and lobbied for it? If not, that may be a sign it is from the Holy.
- Do I feel less anxious and more at peace after living with the message or the response for a time?
- As I live out this response, do I experience more of the gifts of the Holy—love, joy, peace, patience, kindness, goodness, faithfulness, gentleness, self-control?

What about the part of us that questions prayer and thinks of it as a crutch? Some medical research indicates that prayer can make a difference. In *Healing Words,* Larry Dossey (an M.D.) cites several studies, some using humans, others using other organisms. He says prayer has positively affected high blood pressure, wounds, heart attacks, headaches, and anxiety in some human subjects. Other subjects of the studies included water, enzymes, bacteria, fungi, yeast, red blood cells, cancer cells, pacemaker cells, seeds, plants, algae, moth larvae, mice, and chicks. He notes that general prayers, even from a distance, are more effective than specific ones. He calls this discovery the best kept secret in medicine.

Receiving Our Name

The result of taking the wrestling seriously and asking for the angel's gift is to receive a new name, a new self-image. People who have taken this inner journey, who know themselves wholly, experience peace inside, even in the middle of activity or chaos in their lives. Frequently this transformation in self-awareness produces a new, private name or a new personal symbol. Even though people do not talk much about these transformations, I can imagine a few new names that might appear: Speaking Truth, Listener, Soul Builder. It is not important that these names or symbols be public; in fact it is probably better if they are not.

These writers experience their writing as a calling and could not imagine not writing or working on writing in some way. Their trust level is high, because they have experienced first hand the loving guidance of a power greater then they are, who takes them to their core and then back out to the world with great and passionate writing.

These writers can be generous to others, because they do not lose when another writer gains. They can encourage or even give ideas to other writers. Their souls are pulsating with life. They can give generously of their time to encourage and support other writers because they know that the journey of writing takes others to their souls as well.

More than anything, they are unafraid. Their fearlessness is palpable. They can face grief or disappointment or chaos or despondency in others, because they themselves are full: They can encompass the pain of others without taking it on. They are people with grounded centers of strength in the middle of a world of anxiety.

Writers who have wrestled and received their gift often perceive themselves differently ever after. They may see themselves as servants of their work, obedient and faithful followers of their calling, humble and helpful writers whose whole job is to listen to the Holy. Instead of seeing life as a rat race or a grindstone or a stupendous task, they may see it as a dance, in which they take steps in rhythm with the Holy, or move to the music of the spheres. They avoid bumping into people. They lose themselves in the music and movement.

Saint Augustine said, "Learn to dance or the angels won't know what to do with you."

Reflecting on the Chapter

1. Have you received any gifts from your angel yet? What are they?

2. Which is the best way for you to receive the angel's gift: prayer, imagery, or intimacy? Why?

3. What is your name as a writer?

4. Describe your spiritual journey of wrestling with your angel and receiving a gift.

Writing Exercises

1. When I am courageous I write ...

2. If I were unencumbered, I'd write ...

3. My saddest experience was ...

4. My most joyful experience was ...

Visual Exercise

Draw yourself dancing with your angel. What symbols are present?

Visualization

Do the guided imagery found in this chapter, or in your imagination find a reverent place and put your gifts from the angel there. Plan a way to remind yourself of them each time you sit down to write. Write your name on a card and place it among your gifts. Think of this space as holy. Write about this in your journal.

THIRTEEN

～

The Inner Journey: Spiritual Issues of Writers

If we decide to take our spiritual life seriously, amazing things can result in our lives and our writing. The spiritual journey takes us inward, ultimately to a more personal and vulnerable relationship with the Holy. The result is a deepened intimacy, to be sure, but we also move toward an interior freedom, now that we are free of our fearful burdens, which we have never known before.

What stimulates writers to take that inner journey? One writer I know felt blocked in his writing and he was clear that it had nothing to do with technique or discipline or lack of something to say. He'd been published several times and was blocked on his current novel. He thought it had something to do with a deeper dimension of his life, something in the spiritual realm. He sensed he was being confounded in his writing because there was something else for him to pay attention to for the time being, and he wanted to know what that was.

His inner wisdom had guided him well. Something was calling to him from a deeper place. He took the inward journey and it surprised him with twists and turns that took him to a new place in his life and his writing. He began teaching writing and discovered a new calling. His spiritual journey unraveled a mystery that had been building up inside and wanted to be incorporated into his life. He benefited by attending to his spiritual calls, which took him to places he wouldn't have gone himself.

Other writers consider spiritual direction when they are on a plateau in their writing, prolific but unable to break into new territory.

Some writers who work at other things for a living are looking for ways to integrate their writing into their lives more fully. Still others are afraid to change forms or genres, even though they are being called in that direction. Others just want to explore a new arena of their lives, wondering how to integrate their spiritual beings with their everyday lives.

The Process of Deepening

What spiritual issues do people wrestle with as they attend to this inner journey? No one can predict what a given journey will be like, yet certain themes do recur.

Some people enter this journey by engaging with a group of like-minded writers; others read books, write in journals, or find other ways to do it by themselves. Others seek out a spiritual director, a trained spiritual person committed to a listening relationship over time. I have served in that capacity with several writers. In that role, my job is to listen, to ask clarifying questions, to reflect back to them, to support them, and to keep my journey out of theirs. Together we listen for the Holy in their lives, struggling to distinguish their own voice from the Holy's voice and to discern what their heart wants. Whichever method of spiritual deepening you choose, there will be similar issues.

First, let me give you a feel of what the inner journey feels like. For a moment, quiet down and observe your breathing. Ask the Holy to envelope you in a warm white light so you feel safe in this environment. Then allow yourself to be led to that quiet place deep inside you where all is at peace. Stay in that place and be aware that the Holy chooses to dwell in that place within you. Be in the presence of the Holy. Rest and listen. Be grateful. Then slowly come back to the place where you started. Write about the experience in your journal.

Useful places to start on the spiritual journey include the following: telling your own story; examining your image of the Holy; observing your image of self; letting go and asking what your heart wants. That should be enough to keep you going for about ten years. In the early stages of the process, almost everyone feels some resistance. Every time we start along a committed journey to a new place, we find out what is keeping us from going forward. We encounter our inner and outer resistances and get to know them for what they are, not as enemies to be shunned but as friends to be embraced and known. It shocks almost everyone to find that they resist something they want so much.

Resistance comes in the forms of busyness, fear, tardiness, confusion, closing down, getting sick, forgetting, pulling back. Not all resistance is debilitating. Some is a natural way of putting on the brakes so we don't move so fast. Some is a warning sign that the person we are working with is not safe for us. But most resistance is merely the psyche adjusting to the change and checking to see if we are serious about the journey.

Telling Our Story

The single most important element of spiritual deepening is probably for a writer to find a committed spiritual person to listen intently to her story, honor it, and hear it in all its fullness. There is no more sacred ground than honoring a person by listening to her story. And the effect on the teller can be profound, first because she may never have told her story before, and second because no one may have listened so intently before. Committed listening encourages parts of the story that have never been told.

Why is it so important to tell our stories, including our secrets? In *Telling Secrets,* Frederick Buechner says:

> I have come to believe that by and large the human family all has the same secrets, which are both very telling and very important to tell. They are telling in the sense that they tell what is perhaps the central paradox of our condition—that what we hunger for perhaps more than anything else is to be known in our full humanness, and yet that is often just what we also fear more than anything else.
>
> It is important to tell at least from time to time the secret of who we truly and fully are—even if we tell it only to ourselves—because otherwise we run the risk of losing track of who we truly and fully are and little by little come to accept instead the highly edited version which we put forth in hope that the world will find it more acceptable than the real things.
>
> It is important to tell our secrets too because it makes it easier that way to see where we have been in our lives and where we are going. It also makes it easier for other people to tell us a secret or two of their own, and exchanges like that have a lot to do with what being a family is all about and what being human is all about.

In telling yourself your story, a few guidelines may be helpful. Let your inner wisdom guide you in the process. Listen for inner tugs to follow a certain story path, to tell the things you'd forgotten. When you come to places in your story that arouse feeling, allow the feelings to emerge. Remember, you are in a safe relationship with a committed listener. If sadness, joy, fear, anger, tears, or loneliness arise, let them come, and talk about them, if you are able. It helps to use your writing as a support to your inner work; write in your journal, or write poetry, stories, or essays about the experience.

Most people are connected to their spiritual selves when they are in nature or allow themselves quiet, reflective time, but have difficulty connecting their spirituality to their writing or to their everyday life. Sometimes it feels like there is no connection. But this is the heart of spiritual deepening, incorporating spirituality into the stuff of your life and into the heart of your writing.

Some writers get their first insights into the connection between spirituality and life by observing their own writing—by looking at the content of their stories, poems, journals, and nonfiction. If their content or tone is angry, irrational, sexually exploitative, bland, terrorizing, racist, or legalistic, they can see part of themselves emerging. Others observe their characters, who they are and what they do to destroy or support themselves and others. I don't mean that we should leash in our characters, only that we should listen to what our psyche is telling us about our inner life.

One writer always killed off her main characters, although many of them had redeeming experiences along the way. She had asked me to be her listener and reflector, so I asked her if she saw that theme in her own life. She hadn't thought about it but said, "Nothing turns out well in the end, no matter how hard you try." I pondered with her where that philosophy came from, because I sensed it was giving her inner critic a great deal of ammunition. We traced it back to her family, in which the unspoken motto was, "Don't try too hard because it'll backfire." Once she was aware of this, and once she could call on her spiritual side to help her in her writing, she could use both her inner wisdom and help from the Holy to change that script. For starters, she rewrote it in bold words on a piece of paper for the cover of her journal: "Try anything once because it could be fun." Then she began living it out and watching for resistance.

Image of the Holy

A second element in spiritual direction is one's image of the Holy. This is the area in which people seem to have the most energy, both positive and negative. One of the reasons I choose to use synonyms for God, like Holy, the universe, Sophia, higher power, and wisdom, is that I have learned over the years that the term God is loaded with unresolved issues, even for many people within organized religions. Think of your current image of God. Does it change when things aren't going well in your life? Is your God image that of a benevolent father, a magician, a hit-and-run driver, an absentee landlord, a lover, a distant relative, a friend, a banker?

People with negative images of God usually got these in childhood, from their parents or church. A common one is the judgmental, shaming, punishing, old white man with a beard and a stick. Common too is the old white man with a beard who is distant, powerful, and untouchable, especially in times of fear. No wonder so many children love Santa Claus, who is exactly the opposite, but has such similar physical characteristics. Many people inadvertently equate their image of God with their own father. If this relationship was good, their image of God is loving and good, but if it was distant, abusive, or unsafe, God seems the same and it is difficult to establish a close relationship with God. I am never surprised when people say they cannot relate to their childhood image of God.

I encourage people on the spiritual journey to use whatever image of God works for them at the time, as long as they continue to wrestle with the issues involved in that image. Part of the healing process is to let God out of the boxes that God seemed to be in when they were children; to let their image of God develop and grow, not leave it where it was when they were six or ten. Another part of the healing process is to go back and find out where their negative image came from, understand why it was so negative, and work to forgive those who made it so, thus going full circle in the healing process. It is like going back to the scene of the crime to heal the pain.

Many women who have been put down, personally and as a gender, by the authority of their church have a difficult time imagining a masculine image for God that is healing. Using the image of a mother

God, wise woman, Sophia, or goddess can save them from abandoning the spiritual realm altogether. When they heal from the experience of being discounted or spiritually abused, they often add loving masculine images to their Holy female image.

People with positive images of God generally got them in childhood as well. They felt loved, nurtured, and supported by God. They were encouraged for what they did well, not cited for what they did poorly. They were encouraged to be creative and expressive in their love for God. When they want to deepen their spiritual lives, their issues aren't related to their God image but are about how to be closer to God or to listen to God's voice in their lives. For people with no God image at all, the spiritual journey can feel like starting from scratch.

I know a writer who was bottled up because he thought he could only write about certain subjects. He thought not only that other people but that God would punish him if he told his story. He had potent life experiences to relate, both through fiction and nonfiction, but he felt he could only broach safe subjects or he would be ostracized. He had been spiritually and emotionally abused in a strict, fundamentalist church, which told him that God was allergic to him. As a result of spiritual direction, he came to a new image of God and dealt with the truth of his background and with his fear of repercussions. After working through his deep rage, he did a great deal of healing and forgiving. Using a pen name, he was finally able to write about his long history of spiritual abuse, and later was able to write many forms of fiction that were hiding under the stifling weight of his life.

Image of Self

A third element of spiritual deepening is our image of ourselves. It is hard to write freely if we feel like dirt and think that everything we write is worthless. Imagine yourself as a writer and see what comes to mind. Work with that image and see what role your spirituality can play to modify it. The origin of the image is often intertwined with your image of God and with childhood messages. If you were taught that you were bad or guilty or shameful, you probably carry that with you now. So anything you write, no matter how good it is, feels bad.

Improving our image of self is a long and arduous journey and one of the single most important issues that we work on in our lives. I think spiritual deepening gives us clues on how to nurture and know ourselves honestly, without judging ourselves too harshly or letting ourselves off too easily. It is a loving journey of opening to who we really are, being aware of how much we are loved, learning what our life is trying to tell us, and embracing who we are while not acting out our shadows.

A writer who was also a minister asked me to help him get free to write, knowing that he was blocked in his soul. His inner journey brought him to a painful spot, his lifelong struggle with his bisexuality. His journals of twenty years ago reflected his struggle—still unnamed. He made a commitment to the difficult journey of authenticity and spent several years working through the painful issues with his family and his ministry. Slowly he got the acceptance and resolution that he so desperately craved from self and family, and he began to feel the most intense compassion that he had ever felt in his life. He felt whole and wholly loved for the first time.

He felt more free in his writing, and in his teaching was able to broach subjects he never approached before in his work, like spirituality in the workplace. He wrote and taught with great insight and offered profound forgiveness and healing to others. He became a wounded healer.

The central route to self-love, I believe, is understanding deep within ourselves that we are unconditionally loved—loved with no reservations—by the Holy, for who we are. Imagine the difference in your life if you could operate out of a feeling of being loved instead of judged, shamed, hated, pushed, denied, shunned, ignored, or abandoned. Unconditional love: no payments, no expectations, no hoops. It makes all the difference in the world. Just pondering the idea of being loved is a major turning point on the spiritual journey. Accepting love allows us to love ourselves, then to love our neighbors.

When we get to a point of honest self-love and self-responsibility, we free the energy we were using to bottle up our emotions and now can use that energy in our writing. Even the content, technique, and form we choose are freer because we no longer need to live by the strict scripts that were ours before. Spiritual friends and listeners can assist this process powerfully by adding an intimate relationship of support for our self-worth. This holy relationship is one in which we are led with our self doubts to a place of trust and adventure, of daily reaffirmation and courage, of intense love and honesty. We do not lose self-doubt, but when it arises, it tells us that we are losing connection with God and need to concentrate on listening to the Holy and to our soul.

I know of one writer whose self-image is venomous, and it comes through in her writing. She was sexually misused and wounded as a child by a highly intelligent adult male (a God image) and has not resolved the issues. She is technically a superb writer, but every piece she writes includes salacious sex or sensational sexual images not germane to the story. When I hear her stories, well crafted as they are, I am left with the sexual images, which shout out painfully from the story, rather than with the satisfied feeling of a story in which sexuality plays a natural part. It saddens me to read her stories, because I think I know how she would write if she entered a spiritual journey.

Another writer told me this story: He was told by his family that he was not the writer in the family, his father and sister were. Even in high school, when he got awards for his writing and his sister didn't, he was encouraged to give some of the awards to her. Now, after many years of being stuck and not being able to write, he wants to be freed from that family legacy. The power of the family is strong and still hangs over him. For him, a spiritual groundedness will be essential, not only to overcome the strong critic, but to face the wrath of the family when they find out he *is* a writer. He will have more courage to free himself from the grip of the family if he has a deep spiritual base and daily connectedness with the Holy.

What Does Your Heart Want?

A fourth element of spiritual deepening is asking ourselves what our heart most wants. When I bring up that question, I usually get a look of confusion, humor, or blankness. It is not a question that's asked often, and most of us have never thought of the answer. Many of us are not in touch with our heart and don't think we can have what our hearts want anyway. It is too hard, it would cause inconvenience, it is too much to ask, it can't be done, or we don't deserve it.

As we move along on the spiritual journey, the question of what our heart wants becomes more and more important. As we seek the answer, we cut through the static, the family issues, the cultural stresses and expectations, the excuses. We go to our heart, which is where the core of the issue lies. When we are faced with choices, both positive and negative, one way to sort them through is to ask honestly, what does my heart really want? If we are sincere about it and willing to live into the consequences of our heart's desire, it is a powerful question which can guide our lives. Of course, we can deceive ourselves with that question if our egos are still very active or if we are not in close connection with the Holy.

The longer we stay on the journey and desire intimacy with the Holy, the more we can see that what our heart wants at the deepest level is also what the Holy wants for us. We begin to live out our life purpose because we can put aside what our egos want and what our family wants and what our culture wants and what our friends what. We can let ourselves want what the Holy wants for us.

One writer I worked with wanted to write about her African roots and weave the story back into her difficult childhood. She was caught up in the pain of the story and her mixed feelings of self-worth, and was having trouble finishing the book. Despite the fact that she had been accepted for a special writer's program and that an agent liked her work and wanted to see the whole manuscript, she didn't think the agent meant it and so she kept the manuscript and was feeling blocked. When I asked her what she wanted, she said she really wanted to publish this story.

I encouraged her to keep writing and asked if her critic would let her publish the story. She thought about it and said she would talk to her critic. I suggested that the block to finishing the book was inside, and that she needed to keep writing because I knew her heart wanted this. "Face the critic and send the manuscript to the agent," I suggested. "Agents don't ask to see more of a writer's work unless they are interested in it." She listened to her heart, talked to her critic in no uncertain terms, affirmed herself daily, finished the manuscript, put it on a computer, and sent it to the agent. Her heart was satisfied.

Intimacy with the Holy

As the spiritual journey evolves, most writers begin to yearn for a deeper and more intimate relationship with this Holy, who no longer seems capricious, distant, or solely sovereign. This yearning frequently comes as the result of some crisis or knot that we are able to work through in our life, or as a result of not feeling abandoned, or judged, but helped to come to an honest appraisal of self and others.

Intimacy with the Holy comes about in the same way as intimacy with other people, through spending time, talking, listening, being together in crises, working through issues and disagreements, caring for each other, being honest and vulnerable, playing together. I encourage people with whom I journey to keep asking for a deeper relationship with the Holy, and a willingness to do whatever that requires. It usually involves discipline, attentiveness, and risk. It is miraculous, and never dull. Some people are afraid of intimacy with the Holy because they imagine the Holy will ask them to do something they would dread. They can't imagine that a request from the Holy would coincide with their heart's deepest desires.

At its core, spirituality means becoming intimately connected with the Holy and then watching how the Holy takes you to your heart's desire. The catch is that we must seek intimacy before we know exactly where it will take us. Ways to become more intimate include taking walks in nature, asking the Holy to speak directly to us, sitting and observing our life, being quiet, praying, taking sacred baths, inviting the spirit to be within us, entertaining angels, being with loving people, reading holy books, being accountable to another person, going on retreats, having appropriate boundaries, being vulnerable, making sacred space in our lives, slowing down to listen, reaching out to others, accepting our calling, letting the Holy act in our lives—the list goes on and on.

The central struggle in becoming intimate with the Holy is understanding what gets in the way of that intimacy, what separates us from closeness. And that struggle takes us to our core issues: what we worship, where our pain is, and where the healing needs to take place. As a writer, what do you crave? Getting praise? Being published? Writing in a certain form? Using the right words? Getting recognition?

Making money? Are any of these cravings getting in the way of your spirituality? What implications does that have for what you write, how you write, and to whom you write?

Suppose you see your writing as a calling, a passion, coming out of your spiritual groundedness in the Holy. What content would you choose? What form would you choose? Would you find more time to write?

Suppose one person in your life is to be profoundly touched by something you write, but you don't know which person that will be, or which piece of writing. Would anything change? Maybe nothing would change but your intent. Or maybe you'd have more courage; maybe you'd tell a story differently or a character would grow deeper. Maybe your poems would be about people or issues that would make your meaning deeper or your descriptions richer. Maybe your biographies would be about people who have more depth, or your travelogues would include things of the soul.

Intimacy with the Holy is no easy matter. It wrestles its way into your life, and no nook or cranny is off limits. It's like a journey in which you had all the control and now you are voluntarily relinquishing control to a power beyond yourself. Before, this journey was limited by the power of your mind and imagination. Now your journey is unlimited, because your mind and imagination are not in charge. Now the miracles and the adventure begin.

This does not mean your life will be painless and that everything you do will work out. You will have long periods of time—as I have—when you feel you're on a plateau and nothing is happening in your spiritual life. That, too, is part of the journey. Something is happening inside, maybe just a subtle yearning. Or you may experience a dark time, an inner struggle of major proportion, a time of deep spiritual turmoil in which great change occurs. There will be ups and downs, but the miracle will be peace and clarity in the middle of the ups and the downs. The courage and joy that emerge from the pain will be your new companions.

Letting Go

Letting go, or experiencing loving detachment, is an inevitable ingredient of a deepening intimacy with the Holy. People say, "Just let go. Just do it." It all sounds easy, like learning to ride a bike, or learning to write. Don't be fooled. It's not easy. The process of letting go is a life-long commitment.

If you want to find out just how complicated this process is, envision an issue in your life that you feel strongly about: how you want your boss to treat you, or what you want to do on vacation, or what house or apartment you want. Think clearly about what you want, and then imagine letting go and allowing events to go in any direction, including the direction opposite from the one you want. Ouch. Letting go means you can detach from the way decisions go and trust that whatever way they go you will be okay, maybe even better in the long run. You don't do that unless and until you feel you are loved and you understand what it means to be intimate with a loving holy presence.

In writing, I have found it particularly difficult to let go and trust the Holy, because I am so vulnerable when I put my work out in public. If a book goes out of print, how can that possibly be good for me? When I accept the sadness and hurt of that experience and wait to see the bigger picture, including what the book is asking of me, sometimes I can imagine a brighter day.

One of my books went out of print after my co-author died. I was so sad about his death that I could no longer teach with the book or promote it. When it went out of print, I just let it go. Recently, an acquaintance who had watched this process and was supportive of my grief journey took a job as an editor at a publishing house in which books like mine are supported and nourished. She is considering republishing the book, and I am ready to teach the material again. I needed the hiatus to grieve, and now the book can have a new life.

I saw a poster once on an office door which said, "To believe in God is to know that all the rules will be fair and that there will be wonderful surprises." That seemed like the affirmation of someone who had known God intimately, through pain as well as grace. And perhaps that is what the journey is all about after all.

Reflecting on the Chapter

1. How would you describe yourself spiritually?

2. What is your image of the Holy?

3. Have you ever considered greater intimacy with the Holy? Why? Why not?

4. What is your life purpose? How do you live it out?

5. What are the deepest desires of your heart? What is the Holy asking of you?

6. How does your writing reflect your relationship with the Holy?

Writing Exercises

1. The God of my childhood was ...

2. The story of my faith journey is as follows:

3. If I let go, I'm afraid of ...

4. My heart deeply desires ... but if I tell someone, I'm afraid of ...

5. What if the Holy is really ...

Visual Exercise

Draw a symbol of your relationship with the Holy, or of how you would like it to be.

Visualization

Quiet down and go to the calm place inside you. Ask the Holy to draw near and feel the presence come near you. What are your feelings? What is the experience like? Ask for calm and peace to be near the presence. Talk to the Holy. The Holy asks you to follow and you do. You come to a large door and you do not know what is on the other side. The Holy asks you to go through the door. What are you feeling and thinking? Tell the Holy what you are experiencing. What do you decide to do, stay or go through the door? What happens when you do either one? Stay with that experience, knowing that the Holy is there. Come back to this quiet, safe place and write about the experience.

FOURTEEN

≋

Public Crossings

Many people don't feel as if they're really writers unless they've had something published. We, along with our culture, are hard on creative people, insisting on public performance for internal affirmation. When you say you're a writer, people ask, "What have you published?" Madeleine L'Engle's best-selling book, *A Wrinkle In Time*, took ten years to get published. Was she a writer during that time? Was it badly written for nine years before it was published? Or was it so much ahead of its time that no editor could see its potential yet?

Many famous writers have had their work rejected, or worse yet, were told to turn to another field altogether. Flaubert was told that in *Madame Bovary* "you have buried your novel underneath a heap of details which are well done but utterly superfluous." About *The Diary of Anne Frank*, an editor wrote, "The girl doesn't, it seems to me, have a special perception or feeling which would lift that book above the 'curiosity' level." And Rudyard Kipling received the comment, "I'm sorry, Mr. Kipling, but you just don't know how to use the English language."

Making work public can be a treacherous road, disheartening even to the hardiest of writers. And yet it can be the most fulfilling experience of a writer's life. It all depends on the attitude you take and the depth of spirituality you bring to the process.

The transition from private writing to public writing is important; it signifies that the writer and the writing want to be out in the world in some way which includes but is not limited to publishing. You can be a writer and not have anything formally published. Writers are people who write, who think about writing when they are not able to write, and who share their writing with others when they are ready.

I have found a developmental sequence in writers that moves something like this: Writers usually start by writing for themselves. They may write essays, poems, letters to friends and family, journal entries, stories, trip notes, memoirs. At some point, when they want to get more knowledge or encouragement, they make contact with other writers through reading books, taking classes, joining informal groups, or going to writers' workshops. As their confidence grows, they become willing to read their work to others, or to give it to someone else to enjoy or critique.

The more they write and get support and encouragement, the more they are willing to make their work public. This happens in a wide variety of forms, which many writers forget about or skip over in their eagerness to publish. But making work public can include giving our writing as gifts, writing for special events, reading at public gatherings, participating in mentor programs, entering writing competitions, and publishing. When we see our writing as a calling, we go wherever the work and the Holy take us, no matter what form or public crossing that entails.

What Does the Public Crossing Represent?

The public crossing suggests that the writer is willing to let others share his soul, the things he puts on paper, which may come from his inner space in the form of poetry, fiction, or technical material. He is willing to let others people's eyes, ears, and hearts experience his soul, no matter what state that soul is presently in. He is letting his writing go beyond himself, out into the world.

What variety of forms does this public crossing take? I know a woman who writes special poems for family holidays and personal poems for each child in her family. Do those poems need to be formally published to be well written? Would it even make sense to publish them? Probably not.

Other people write for social or community events. My 25th college reunion committee sponsored a limerick writing contest, and entries came in from across the country. Here are a few examples of the wit and humor of unpublished poets. The college, Saint Olaf, has Scandinavian roots, which are crucial to understanding some of the limericks.

As an Ole, I booked by the hour,
Learning knowledge is ultimate power,
Now I know, looking back,
That it's true, for a fact—
That we lived in an Ivory Tower!
    Carol

With Thorson and Johnson to teach me,
A lim'rick was not out of reach—gee,
But where are they now
That I forgot how—
Come help me you guys, I beseech ye!
    Susan

The clues, well I guess they are there,
Little paunch, blurry vision, less hair,
And then there is Clinton
The signs clearly hintin'
We're adults, what a bummer, no fair!
    Ron

Two young people, Ole en Lena,
As freshmen vore little green beana.
Dey met very soon
As dey vatched Brigadoon
Uffda, um yah yah, vat a scena.
    Judy

One of the most joy-filled experiences in my writing career has been the annual holiday piece that I give to my friends as a gift. Each year, I wonder what it will be and what my theme will be. About Halloween time, I receive the theme for that holiday season from the Holy, and then I wait to see what creative expression will evolve. One year I drew a picture; other years I wrote a fantasy about the origin of the star of Bethlehem, an historical essay asking what would have happened if the wise men had been women, and a memoir about healing my dread of the holidays. Now my holiday piece is the grounded center around which my entire holiday season revolves, and it makes the holidays not only more enjoyable but much less stressful.

Some writers specialize in the fine practice of letter writing, which is rapidly becoming a lost art. I have a friend who has been writing to his college roommate for fifty years, and the letters I receive from him are the most enjoyable writing I have ever read. Sometimes private letters make a further transformation and are collected into books such as, the letters of E. B. White.

Other writers use their gifts to write humorous pieces for events like retirement parties or organizational celebrations. These pieces give joy and laughter to the listener and satisfaction to the writer. Would that we had more artistic components to public celebrations. Think of how the country responded to Maya Angelou's poem at President Clinton's inauguration. Yet most such pieces are almost never published. Does that reflect the seriousness of the writer or the quality of the writing? In most cases, I think not. Some writing is simply not intended for publication.

Having said all that, there are times when writing needs to make the public crossing to a wider audience than it can reach through the author's distribution alone. That audience can be reached through professional journals, newsletters, instructional books, letters to the editor, videos and television productions, as well as publishing in books and magazines. The list goes on and on. The appropriate public forum is not the same for every piece.

The Journey of Publication

Many books have been written about publishing, covering the how-tos and the must-nots. I will not attempt to cover the same ground. But I do want to share with you my attitude toward publication, because it has given me hope, grounding, and personal satisfaction over the years I have been writing.

My overall philosophy is this: Each writing piece has wisdom instilled within it. It knows how and whether it wants to be published. Our job is to listen to the piece, keep our egos out of the process, and let the Holy work in us to support the writing.

I have also evolved five principles of publishing. The first is that we need to develop a relationship with our writing and ask it to lead us, to tell us what it wants from us.

This process starts long before the piece is ready for publication. For me, it starts when I consider new topics to write on. Some people look at the market to see what is selling and let that determine what they write. Others query the market with ideas to see what magazines or publishers will take. Both of these work, especially if your interest and the market's coincide. What I do is ask my soul what is brewing there and what I have energy for. I ask what my passion is at this time and what I am willing to write boldly about.

As a result, not only am I eager to write, and willing to stay with the piece long enough to get it published, but I find that what is in my soul is more likely to attract readers than any market-driven piece I could write. My writing is deeper, more passionate, more vulnerable, and more compelling when I write from my soul.

This idea is not new. In the 1600s, a Chinese artist, Kung Hsien, wrote:

> Nowadays when people paint they only do what appeals to the
> common eye;
> I alone do not seek to please the present,
> I note this with a laugh.

A writing student of mine, Joan, has developed her own philosophy of writing and publishing.

> [One] thing that helps me is the notion of "my job/not my job." It is my job to write. It is my job to put it out there. It is not my job to accept or reject my pieces. It is not my job to run a magazine or a publishing company ... If I have done my writing practice and my marketing practice, I have done my job. What happens after that is not up to me ... I affirm that good writing is never wasted. Often I believe, though I have absolutely nothing to substantiate this, that it changes the quality of the universe ever so slightly. A vainglorious proposition, but how are we to do good work against such odds if we are not vainglorious occasionally?

My second principle is that we need to find our own niche in writing. Some people write well as long as they stay under five pages, but they get bogged down in longer pieces. I find it almost impossible to say anything in less than two pages. This became clear to me when I took a short story class, in which we were asked to stay under 500 words. I admire writers who can be that pithy.

The problem is that many writers think their own best form must be the wrong form or it wouldn't come so easily. People who write short pieces think they should be writing books. People who write fiction think they should be writing poetry. The spiritual principle is to write what is given to you as part of who you are and what your soul wants to write, no matter what that is. It is part of the journey of self-acceptance and faithfulness. It doesn't mean you'll never switch forms, but that when you switch it will be because you are led to do so, and not out of disgust for your writing.

My third principle is that we need to let our lives feed the work while we are writing and not rush ourselves to finish, thus missing some richness that could change, nourish, or challenge the work. I don't like to write to deadlines, although I know other writers who can only write that way. I set my own deadlines and I am usually right on target.

My fourth principle is that we need to decide whether or not we can live on royalties or fees. I do not depend on the money from books to make a living. If I did, I would have to take on projects I should never consider. I do make a living indirectly from my books, but I depend on public speaking and seminars rather than royalties. I consider finances a large part of my faith journey. If I write what I am called to write, I have found that the money works itself out. I'm not rich, but I am exceedingly satisfied and have peace about my life and work.

In my experience, most writers make a living doing work other than writing. They write on the side because of the love of writing and the creative outlet it provides. Other writers' journeys take them in the opposite direction—toward depending on magazine and feature writing, or novels and nonfiction books. Either approach is fine, as long as you have considered it as part of your spiritual journey. What matters is having the faith to accept whatever way is best for you.

My fifth principle is that we need to approach the publication process as part of the spiritual journey. This is the most difficult part of the whole writing process for most writers. I have had a lot of experience and I still find it cumbersome to send my work out. Published writers will tell you that what one editor loves another one will dislike. An editor's opinion is not related only to your writing style, but to your content, timeliness, reputation, geographical location, gender (ask George Elliot about that one), network, ability to sell books, and so on.

With all those variables, how can you ever expect to get anything published? That is why you have to see the process as a spiritual journey, believing that your book already knows where it will go and that your job is to support it.

Making Contacts for Your Work

The route to publishing varies depending on your type of writing, but let's examine book publishing as one form. Most writers don't have book publishers calling them. How do they make publishing contacts? Some query the publisher before they write. Others send their work to publishers over the transom, with no prior contact. Still others use a network of writers in order to get names of editors or publishers. Some use agents; some don't. Writers who have published can use their own publishers as part of a network. People who self-publish do not need these networks but need distribution contacts. I have used most of these methods of publishing, and in my experience no one way is better than the others. It depends on the piece and the goal of the writer.

A personal contact is still the easiest way to get published. There is no substitute for knowing someone who can introduce your work to an editor. But how do you get to know editors, especially if you've never published before? Writing classes are good places to build a network, since other writers and the teacher may have good contacts. The same is true of writers' conferences, where editors and agents appear, scouting for new and talented writers.

To narrow down the list of publishers to those most likely to publish your work, go to your favorite bookstore and find the section that includes books like the one you are writing. Open the front covers of the books most like yours and write down publishers, editors, and agents. (Just look at the cover page and the acknowledgments, where authors sometimes thank these people). Then go to the library and find a book that lists publishers, addresses, editors, and the types of books they publish. Either send your manuscript directly to these people or make contact with people in your network who may know them.

When I do this, I keep talking to the Holy and asking the book where it wants to go, and I follow the urges I experience. Being willing to acknowledge my fear helps keep the process from becoming overwhelming. Most people are afraid to make their work public, so talking about it with another writer helps immensely.

The Perilous Journey of Publishing

It takes a lot of courage to put work out there for the world to critique, judge, praise, and publish or not publish. We experience the parts of ourselves that are fearless, daring, cowardly, scared. We face some perilous times, some strong winds and storms, and also some gentle breezes and calm fulfillment. It is an adventure. If you get discouraged easily, it may not be for you.

To show you a sampling of the ups and downs of the publishing process, let me tell you a brief tale of my books and their journeys. Each book had a different process, and each book told me what it wanted by refusing to go in directions that were not appropriate.

When a door closes, I listen. But I do not give up. I ask what it means, and then go in the direction that suggests. I believe that writing takes on a life of its own, and I speak of it in that way, even though it sounds strange to some people. I believe the work becomes real and full of life, and that it is very much a part of the ongoing process if we let it be.

My first book contract came as a result of making contact with an editor at a conference in which books were exhibited to conference participants. Another book was published through my co-author's network. Still another was published by a local women's organization through a fundraising effort. I used an agent once because someone connected me with her; another time, I used my publishing contacts from an earlier book. There is no secret, no magic way. It is a matter of believing in your work and persisting, sometimes for years. That has been especially true with one of my books. Let me tell you that story.

It was my second book, *Real Power*, and it took me three years to write, because so much of my soul went into the writing. When I approached my previous publisher with the manuscript, they weren't interested—much to my chagrin. One of the editors had moved to a new press in the meantime, which is not unusual, and he called me to see if I wanted to publish with them. A small publisher in Minneapolis had also heard about the manuscript as a result of my speeches and had asked to see it when I was done. I had forgotten about the smaller press and had an unsigned contract in hand from the larger publisher, which I was uneasy about because mine would be one of their first trade books. I was ready to sign with this larger publisher when I went to a fund-raiser and bumped into the publicist for the local publisher.

She asked if I had finished the manuscript and I said that I was ready to sign a contract. She said, "We've been waiting for you to send it to us. Can we just have a chance to see it before you sign the contract?" I said they could and two days later the book let me know in no uncertain terms that it wanted to go with the local publisher. I felt that the book was home. The smaller publisher convinced me they loved the book and would do more for it than the big publisher would. It was a difficult decision. My book got lots of personal attention and a few years later the publisher was bought out by a larger, well-known press.

The book sold steadily and well for several years, then out of the blue I got a letter from the publisher saying it was going out of print. I was shocked, especially since they were eagerly reviewing another of my manuscripts. When I cooled down and called my editor, I found out it was a mistake. An intern has inadvertently sent out the letter. However, a few years later, while the book was still selling steadily and well, I got another letter saying they were letting the book go out of print. This time they meant it.

I decided it was not time for this book to die, so I went back to my first publisher and asked if they were willing to reissue the book. They said yes, and we spent nine months working on rewrites and doing marketing plans. They were due to send me the contract when I got a letter instead saying they had reorganized and would not be publishing it after all. I was devastated. I thought this was the final blow, so I decided to treat the process reverentially. I had a private funeral for my book, wrote soothing and thankful words to it in my journal, and gently put it in the farthest corner of a cupboard in my office. I thought it was over. My book didn't.

Several months later, after the book had been out of print for two years, I felt a nagging in my mind after a friend mentioned a publisher who specialized in out-of-print books. I wondered if this was wishful thinking or whether I needed to pursue it. Would I be disappointed again? This book had already been seriously considered by three publishers. I waited. The thoughts didn't go away. The ideas in the book grew more powerful in my mind.

I finally made an overture to the publisher of out-of-print books, thinking of this as my last resort. I got an enthusiastic response and even an agreement to add my latest chapter on leadership, which I had been working on for five years. But the press was small, and distribution would be a problem. I thought about it and decided to do it, because I felt strongly that this book was not finished saying what it had to say. The book is back in print and is getting into the right hands. It is happy. I am happy. The publisher is happy. We have all found the right home. And this whole journey took fourteen years.

The thing I want to stress is that there is no one way to make the public crossing; the journey is what is important. Listen to your work; listen to your heart; listen to the Holy. Listen for the form your work wants to take and the way in which it wants to be public. It took courage to put my book away and think of never seeing it in print again. And after two years of its being out of print, it took courage to dig deep for the energy to send it out once again. I felt that I was being asked to serve the book, to nurture it once more, to believe that it was not finished. Maybe our writing has a life of its own and knows more than we do. Our real work may be to listen to it.

Reflecting on the Chapter

1. What is your motto for your writing?

2. What, if anything, is keeping you from the public side of writing?

3. What is the most interesting form of public writing for you? Why?

4. What are your publishing and writing principles?

Writing Exercises

1. The first thing I will publish (or my next piece of published writing) will be ...

2. I love my writing for these reasons ...

3. Success for me as a writer is ...

4. If money were no object I would write ...

5. An affirmation for my writing is ...

Visual Exercise

Make a collage of your writing—past, present, and future.

Visualization

Imagine that you could publish whatever your heart desires. Family and friends are at a party for you, a public reading of your published work. As you read, you look at the faces in the room. Who is pleased? Who is not pleased? Go to a quiet place inside you and reflect on why the listeners are pleased or not. Come back to the room you are in and write about this reflection in your journal.

FIFTEEN

The Writer's Soul Meets the World

In *Wishful Thinking*, Frederick Buechner describes vocation (from the Latin *vocare*, meaning "to call"), as "the place where your deep gladness and the world's deep hunger meet." He goes on to say that this may not be as simple as it looks. A doctor who is working on disease control but who hates her work is not exercising vocation. Neither is a marketing director who loves his work marketing deodorant products.

Why do you write? Do you write to express yourself, to make money, to become well known, to educate others?

When we view writing as a spiritual process in which our soul is intricately involved, we see that writing is indeed a calling, a vocation. We are led to our vocation by the Holy, visited and empowered by our angel who requires us to wrestle to receive our gift. And our writing is bumped to and fro by our critic, who wants to destroy our writing but whom we can embrace and use appropriately to make our writing better. It was part of the plan all along, this calling of ours, just waiting for us to wake up and notice it.

The difficulty for some of us was that we thought learning the craft of writing was enough. Much to our dismay, we learned that the angel wanted to wrestle us to the ground and make us sit in dark places for uncomfortable periods of time while we came to terms with our darkness, our shadows, ourselves, our core. Out of that wrestling came a unique gift from the angel and a sense of soaring, or internal freedom, perhaps for the first time in our lives—the soul set free.

When the soul is free, it frequently offers an unusual, grateful response. With freedom comes a new capacity, not just to be a good writer, not just to make money or be well known, not just to entertain, enrich, or inspire others. The freed soul has a natural inclination to reach out to other writers, to the community, and to the world.

A useful analogy is that of death and resurrection. You've met your death, been in the tomb for a long time in the quiet of your soul, and now it is the frightening time to re-emerge and do the rest of the magnificent work. It's not over when you let your writing take you to your core and find your truth. It's just beginning. Coming out of your core of pain is your passion, your light, your healing. The writing that emerges may include more compelling content, exceptional characters, courageous risks in structure, breaks with tradition, genuine care about the world around you, mentoring, volunteering. What matters is to feel it and to follow it instead of being afraid.

Parker Palmer, in a wonderful book about the spiritual life, *The Active Life,* has a chapter called "Threatened With Resurrection." The title alone is challenging. Yet he is right. Many people fear life itself more than they fear death in its various forms. They are threatened by interior freedom, the loss of heaviness, the absence of depression, the soul's free flight. It is easier to stay in the tomb. Coming out of the tomb may mean being more public with our passion than we are comfortable with, or becoming leaders in ways we never dreamed of.

Palmer says it best in his own words: "No wonder resurrection is so threatening; it forces us to abandon any illusion we may have that we are in charge of our own lives, able to do whatever we want, accountable to no one but ourselves, free of responsibility to others. Resurrection requires that we replace that illusion with the reality that we rise and fall together, that we have no choice but to live in and with and for the entire community of creation."

What kind of leadership does this new freedom call us to? Palmer helps us again with his description of great leadership in *Leading From Within*: "Great leadership comes from people who have made that downward journey through violence and terror, who have touched that deep place where we are in community with each other, and who can help take other people to that place. That is what great leadership is all about."

What would leadership in writing be?

First, I think all writers, especially those who have taken a serious spiritual journey, have the responsibility to mentor other writers. I am indebted to two writing mentors. One was Brenda Ueland, whom I only met once but whose words are still indelibly marked on my brain: "Never be afraid. Never."

My other mentor was a man named John Mihelic, who worked with me on one article for several months. It was my first venture beyond academic writing, and I was in my mid-twenties. He taught me three things that I remember: Write the way you speak; use active language; and say what you want to say up front and boldly instead of hiding it on page twelve. He also helped me gain the thing I needed most in order to write—confidence.

Second, writers have a responsibility to listen to their calling, because each person has a unique role to fill in the world. Third, writers have a responsibility to stay close to their center so they can remain grounded in the Holy and not be swayed easily by the whims or fears of the day. Courageous leaders live on the edge, beyond the fear of the resurrection. Oddly enough, it is absolutely critical that you stay close to the center if you want to live on the edge.

Let's go back to the Writer's Wheel just to get some examples of leadership that could emerge through the various writing forms. I'm not suggesting that everything we write needs to follow these guidelines, but that we stop to think about why and how we choose the approach we do, and how we are moving back into the world. Each writer will find her own unique way if she desires it.

Instructional writers could be aware that the knowledge they write about is indeed useful to the world and can further a just cause. Religious writers could work toward tolerance and peace. An example in this category is *Silent Spring,* by Rachel Carson, which alerted the world to the misuse of the environment and the dangers of industrial chemicals.

Inspirational writers could write biographies of people who were courageous and made a significant difference in other people's lives.

Travelogues could dig deeper into the cultures they touch and cover meatier material. Memoirs could be more vulnerable, giving us glimpses into interior space. Thomas Keneally's *Schindler's List* is an example of this kind of work. When you read the book or see the movie and learn what this one man did to save so many Jews from the Holocaust, it encourages you to ask yourself, "How can I have a meaningful life by doing something that makes a difference to someone else?"

Fanciful writing could touch our subconscious with stories and fables that reach archetypal levels. They could send us to redemptive places, inside and outside. Science fiction could leave us with hope for the future. In this category, I think of C.S. Lewis's *Narnia Chronicles* or Lewis Carroll's *Alice in Wonderland,* where we not only see a wide array of characters, but these characters are metaphors for us.

Entertaining writing could be much more than solid technique. It could give us stories that would make our hearts soar, our spirits rise, our souls glow from the courage of people and the love of life. A very sobering but enlightening book in this category is *Imagining Argentina,* by Lawrence Thornton, a riveting story of life and death in a repressed culture, and of the hundreds of mothers in Argentina who continue to march for their missing children.

Personal writers could allow themselves to be vulnerable and accessible so we could learn from their courage. They could make their journals available, in all their rawness, so the stuff of life would be revealed. They could bring back the fine art of letter writing and make it part of our fabric again. The journals of May Sarton come to mind, especially *Journal of a Solitude,* in which she chronicles her daily activities, her thoughts and feelings on subjects from the intimate and sublime to the mundane.

Persuasive writers could use their images to help stop violence and pornography and abuse. Criticism could be honest and down to earth, and include sensitive alternatives. Journalists could write about the things that elevate the human spirit in addition to covering tragedies like fires and murders. Betty Friedan's *The Feminine Mystique* is an example. The book lit a fire under a generation of women who had not been aware of their options before—and she helped start the women's movement.

Listening to the Holy

When we begin to listen to the Holy on the issue of writing as a vocation, not only does our writing change, but the way we see ourselves as writers changes too. This soul emergence is absorbed into other areas of our lives as well. These are some ways writers have chosen to live out the meaning of vocation in their writing careers.

- Some writers teach writing principles to others, especially to those who could not afford to take regular classes. They make it a point to be supportive teachers, not assuaging their own egos, but waiting for what the students have to teach them. One woman I know runs a poetry group at a women's prison. She teaches from her soul by listening to the messages in the poetry that emerges, honoring the feelings and encouraging further expression.

- Another published writer makes a point to respond to everyone who writes him about his books. He is generous, open, and helpful to other writers in his feedback. In fact, he has a running dialogue with several writers. He considers it part of his writing mission to support other writers.

- Some writers dedicate a certain percent of their royalties to meaningful groups or projects so that their writing goes beyond itself and its content. A few well-known writers donate all the royalties from specific projects to certain passions or causes.

- Some writers mentor two or three younger writers seriously and for no pay. They stay with them, write to them, meet with them, encourage them, make them feel worthwhile, especially when they are down on themselves, help them remember what it felt like to be unconditionally loved by someone older and more experienced.

- Some writers use their best writing skills to work on issues they are drawn to. Some organize writing groups or readings for homeless writers. Some help publish their work. They listen and learn, and sometimes it changes their world. My friend who was raped twelve years ago is not only talking about it after a long silent time, but is now writing a memoir to help other rape victims who have silenced themselves.

- Some writers work on issues within the world's writing community. Many writers are being silenced for their writing; other writers are working to free them.

- Some writers volunteer to edit newsletters for their favorite organizations.
- Some writers make themselves available as spiritual companions to writers who need someone who understands and is farther along on the journey.
- Some writers take a risk by writing about topics the world may not be ready for, because the world may need to hear about them now, before the time is right.
- Some writers write letters to people who would benefit from their support: to other writers, editors, publishers, agents. They encourage them and thank them for what they are doing. They write from their souls without any expectations. They may touch a life, or even save one, in this way.
- Some writers take risks in their jobs as technical or public writers. They put more of their souls into their writing and watch for the results. The speech writer I mentioned earlier did this. When she had the courage to write speeches using her power and passion, the speeches got picked up by wire services all over the state. Now her boss is interested in the topic she was passionate about and planned a seminal conference on the topic. Her writing made a difference.

A word of caution: Don't spend all your energy trying to do the things I'm suggesting here if you have not yet done any of the soul work described earlier. You will burn out, get mad if things don't work out, seek recognition for the effort, or get discouraged. The generosity and responsibility I'm describing come from a liberated soul that does not see this as duty but as a grateful response.

Writing is a vocation, a calling. The Holy is waiting to take your writing and your soul to the new place of freedom. Heed the call.

Reflecting on the Chapter

1. Have you ever experienced your writing as a calling? Describe how this feels to you.

2. What is your vocation?

3. What does resurrection mean to you? Is it threatening?

4. Who is your mentor? What does that person do to help you?

5. Where do you feel led to in your writing life now?

6. What does it mean to you that you have to stay close to the center if you want to live on the edge?

Writing Exercises

1. My most sacred experience was ...

2. When I experience my writing as a calling, I wonder ...

3. Advice I'd like to give other writers is ...

4. Advice I need from other writers is ...

5. As a result of reading this book, I think of success in writing as ...

Visual Exercise

Draw and write your calling as a writer in the form of a picture or plaque with a frame. What does it mean to you?

Guided Imagery

Be quiet in a safe place in your center. A wise figure comes to you as if it were the middle of the night and wakes you from sleep. The figure puts an object at your feet and you pick it up. It is a book containing only two pages. You open the book and on the first page is the title "The World's Deep Hunger." The figure asks you to write what you think that is under the title. You do so. What do you write? Then the figure asks you to turn to the second page. It is entitled, "My Deep Gladness." Again, the figure asks you to write what that is on the page beneath the title. What do you write? Then the figure closes the book and you notice your name is on the front of the book but there is no title. The figure asks you to write a title. What do you write? What meaning does this book have for you? What difference will it make in your writing and your life?

BIBLIOGRAPHY

Barry, William, and William Connolly. *The Practice of Spiritual Direction*. Seabury, 1982.

Burnham, Sophy. *A Book of Angels*. New York: Ballantine Books, 1990.

Cameron, Julia. *The Artist's Way: A Spiritual Path to Higher Creativity*. New York: Jeremy P. Tarcher, Perigee, 1992.

Campbell, Joseph. *The Power of Myth*. New York: Doubleday, 1988.

Dillard, Annie. *The Writing Life*. New York: Harper & Row, 1989.

_____. *Teaching a Stone to Talk*. New York: Harper Collins, 1988

Dossey, Larry, M.D. *Healing Words: The Power of Prayer and the Practice of Medicine*. San Francisco: HarperCollins, 1993.

Duerk, Judith. *Circle of Stones*. San Diego: LuraMedia, 1991.

_____. *I Sit Listening to the Wind*. San Diego: LuraMedia, 1993.

Dyckman, Katherine, and Patrick L. Carroll. *Inviting the Mystic, Supporting the Prophet*. New York: Paulist Press, 1981.

Eisler, Riane. *The Chalice and the Blade*. San Francisco: Harper & Row, 1987.

Elbow, Peter. *Writing Without Teachers*. New York: Oxford University Press, 1973.

Eliot, T. S. *The Complete Poems and Plays*. New York: Harcourt, Brace & World, 1962.

Estes, Clarissa Pinkola. *The Creative Fire*. Boulder, Colo.: Sounds True Recordings, 1991.

_____, *Women Who Run With the Wolves*. New York: Ballantine, 1992.

Faraday, Ann. *The Dream Game*. New York: Perennial Library, 1976.

Fischer, Kathleen. *Women at the Well: Feminist Perspectives on Spiritual Direction*. New York: Paulist Press, 1988.

Friedman, Bonnie. *Writing Past Dark*. New York: HarperCollins, 1993.

Galland, China. *Longing for Darkness*. New York: Viking, 1990.

Gardner, John. *Self-Renewal*. New York: Harper & Row, 1964.

Goldberg, Natalie. *Writing Down the Bones*. Boston: Shambhala, 1986.

Goldman, Karen. *Angel Voices*. New York: Simon & Schuster, 1993.

Gorsuch, John. *An Invitation to the Spiritual Journey*. New York: Paulist Press, 1990.

Gray, Elizabeth. *Sacred Dimensions of Women's Experience*. Wellesley: Roundtable, 1988.

Hagberg, Janet. *Real Power*. Salem, Wis.: Sheffield Publishing, 1994.

_____, and Richard Leider. *The Inventurers*. Reading, Mass.: Addison Wesley, 1986.

Harris, Maria. *Dance of the Spirit*. New York: Bantam, 1989.

Kelsey, Morton, and Barbara Kelsey. *Sacrament of Sexuality*. Warwick, N.Y.: Amity House, 1986.

Klinkenborg, Vernon. *The Last Fine Time*. New York: Vintage, 1990.

L'Engle, Madeleine. *Walking on Water: Reflections on Faith and Art*. Wheaton, Ill.: Harold Shaw, 1980.

Leonard, Linda. *Wounded Woman*. Boston: Shambhala, 1982.

Lloyd, Roseann. *Tap Dancing for Big Mom*. Saint Paul: New Rivers, 1985.

Lloyd, Roseann, and Richard Solly. *Journey Notes: Writing for Recovery and Spiritual Growth*. Center City, Minn.: Hazelden Books, 1989.

Mason, Marilyn. *Making Our Lives Our Own*. San Francisco: HarperCollins, 1991.

May, Gerald. *Care of Mind/Care of Spirit: Psychiatric Dimensions of Spiritual Direction*. San Francisco: Harper & Row, 1982.

Miller, William. *Your Golden Shadow*. San Francisco: HarperCollins, 1989.

Moore, Thomas. *Care of the Soul*. New York: HarperCollins, 1992.

Nouwen, Henri. *With Open Hands*. Notre Dame, Ind.: Ave Maria, 1972.

Palmer, Parker. *The Active Life.* San Francisco: HarperCollins, 1990.

———. *Leading From Within: Reflections on Leadership and Spirituality.* Indianapolis IN: Indiana Office of Campus Ministries, 1990.

Olsen, Tillie. *Silences.* New York: Dell, 1978.

Perera, Sylvia. *Descent to the Goddess.* Toronto: Inner City Books, 1981.

Rico, Gabriele. *Writing the Natural Way.* Los Angeles: Jeremy P. Tarcher, 1983.

Rilke, Ranier Maria. *Letters to a Young Poet.* New York: Random House, 1984.

Rupp, Joyce. *The Star in My Heart.* San Diego: LuraMedia, 1989.

Sanford, John. *Dreams and Healing.* Ramsey, N.J.: Paulist Press, 1978.

Savary, Louis, Patricia Berne and Strephon Williams. *Dreams and Spiritual Growth.* New York: Paulist Press, 1984.

Siegel, Bernie, M.D. *Love, Medicine and Miracles.* New York: Harper & Row, 1986.

Sinetar, Marsha. *Ordinary People as Monks and Mystics.* New York: Paulist Press, 1986.

———. *Do What You Love, the Money Will Follow.* New York: Paulist Press, 1987.

Sternburg, Janet. *The Writer on Her Work.* Volume II. New York: W.W. Norton, 1991.

Ueland, Brenda. *If You Want To Write: A Book About Art, Independence and Spirit.* Saint Paul: Graywolf, 1987.

Underhill, Evelyn. The Life of the Spirit and the Life of Today. San Francisco: HarperCollins, 1986.

Vander Vort, Kay, Joan Timmerman and Eleanor Lincoln. *Walking in Two Worlds.* Saint Cloud, Minn.: North Star, 1992.

Wall, Steve, and Harvey Arden. *Wisdom Keepers.* Hillsboro, Ore.: Beyond Words Publishing, 1990.

Welty, Eudora. *One Writer's Beginnings.* Cambridge, Mass.: Harvard University Press, 1984.

Woodman, Marion. *The Pregnant Virgin.* Toronto: Inner City Books, 1985.

Woolfe, Virginia. *Women and Writing*. New York: Harcourt Brace
    Jovanovich, 1979.
Zinsser, William. *On Writing Well*. New York: Harper & Row, 1980.

About the Author

Janet O. Hagberg teaches writing at the Loft, the largest non-profit literary organization in the United States. A certified spiritual director and nationally acclaimed speaker, she is the author of four books including the bestseller, *The Inventurers: Excursions in Life and Career Renewal*. Her philosophy of life is "if you don't learn how to laugh at yourself, sooner or later someone else will." Ms. Hagberg lives in Minneapolis.